Cally Parkinson has combined brilliant resea[...] heart of transforming a church! In *Rise: Bola [...] Church*, Cally gives you a design that will revolutionize your church to be all that God meant for it to be. Who doesn't want that? This is a must read for every church leader.

> **DAVE FERGUSON**
> Lead pastor of Community Christian Church and author of *Finding Your Way Back to God*

Filled with case studies and strategies for the transformation of your church, *Rise* is a powerful tool for leaders and congregations who want more of Christ in their church. Based on research and real examples, *Rise* charts the pathway to change and church renewal. The REVEAL survey proved that not every church that grows is spiritually strong. *Rise* reveals ways to strengthen your church based on its unique characteristics.

> **C. JEFFREY WRIGHT, JD, MBA**
> Chief executive officer of UMI (Urban Ministries, Inc.)

Church leaders looking for next steps for moving their congregations to new levels of church health and ministry effectiveness will find *Rise* to be an exceptional resource. This book provides answers to the unique needs of several church types. The research will enable you to identify your church's unique path to greater vitality. I highly recommend *Rise* to all churches desiring to attain greater ministry impact.

> **TODD HUDNALL, DMin**
> Lead pastor of Radiant Church and author of *Church, Come Forth*

Rise is a win for the body of Christ! We think every pastor and church leader should read this helpful resource, just as every church benefits from taking the REVEAL assessment. *Rise* takes the snapshot of church spiritual health from REVEAL and puts legs and action to it. It combines great hope, biblical direction, and practical suggestions every church can use.

> **ROY and MARGARET FITZWATER**
> Coaches, consultants, and co-directors of Navigator Church Ministries

Rise is a clear and inspiring call to action. The archetype descriptions reflect an excellent balance of candor and grace. We see our parishes in them, and they challenge us to courageously recalibrate towards spiritual growth. A wonderful answer to the "what do we do now?" question.

> **RT. Rev. MARIANN EDGAR BUDDE, BISHOP, and Ms. JOEY RICK**
> Canon for Congregational Vitality, the Episcopal Diocese of Washington

This is a terrific volume, full of wisdom and practical advice about strategies to move churches along the path to greater vibrancy. Convinced that all churches have the power to thrive spiritually but eschewing a "one size fits all" strategy, Cally assesses the challenges eight church "archetypes" face and the ways in which they can achieve or sustain spiritual depth. This is a truly hopeful book, based as it is on the conviction that all churches can grow spiritually, no matter where they fall on the spectrum of vitality. It could be profitably read by every pastor in America.

BILL SIMON
Founder of Parish Catalyst and coauthor of *Living the Call*

As a Lutheran pastor and consultant to mainline congregations, I recognize many of the archetypes in this book. But the important thing is not just more diagnoses of the problem—we have lots of books about that already. This book looks at strategies that have helped move churches forward and gives real guidance for leaders who want to do more than simply wallow in their situations.

DAVE DAUBERT, DMin, PhD
Parish pastor and lead consultant for Day 8 Strategies; author of *Seeing Through New Eyes* and *Lutheran Trump Cards*

The three questions a church must ask at the onset of a renewal journey are "Who are we?" "Where are we headed?" and "How will be get there?" When congregations ask and answer those questions, they will have stepped onto the path of renewal. Until now there have been few comprehensive tools to help churches wrestle with those basic questions. *Rise*, especially when accompanied with REVEAL survey results, is that comprehensive tool and should be foundational reading for congregations seeking revitalization.

DR. KEITH DOORNBOS
Director of the Renewal Lab at Calvin Seminary

The work of revitalizing the church has just taken a remarkable step forward with *Rise*! This challenging endeavor requires a clear and straightforward understanding of the current reality facing a church. God is clearly moving across the US, bringing revival to the Christian church, and the breakthrough notion of church archetypes will empower this work for years to come.

T. GREG SURVANT
Cofounder and managing partner of Spiritual Leadership, Inc.; former vice president and general manager of Lexmark International, Inc.

RISE

BOLD STRATEGIES TO TRANSFORM YOUR CHURCH

CALLY PARKINSON
WITH NANCY SCAMMACCA LEWIS

NAVPRESS

*A NavPress resource published in alliance
with Tyndale House Publishers, Inc.*

NAVPRESS⬤®

NavPress is the publishing ministry of The Navigators, an international Christian organization and leader in personal spiritual development. NavPress is committed to helping people grow spiritually and enjoy lives of meaning and hope through personal and group resources that are biblically rooted, culturally relevant, and highly practical.

For more information, visit www.NavPress.com.

Rise: Bold Strategies to Transform Your Church

Copyright © 2015 by Tango XVII, LLC. All rights reserved.

A NavPress resource published in alliance with Tyndale House Publishers, Inc.

NAVPRESS and the NAVPRESS logo are registered trademarks of NavPress, The Navigators, Colorado Springs, CO. *TYNDALE* is a registered trademark of Tyndale House Publishers, Inc. Absence of ® in connection with marks of NavPress or other parties does not indicate an absence of registration of those marks.

The Team:
  Don Pape, Publisher
  Caitlyn Carlson, Acquisitions Editor

Designed by Dean H. Renninger

Cover illustration copyright © torokimola/DollarPhotoClub. All rights reserved.

Cataloging-in-Publication Data is available.

ISBN 978-1-63146-440-9

Printed in the United States of America

21	20	19	18	17	16	15
7	6	5	4	3	2	1

ALSO BY CALLY PARKINSON

Reveal: Where Are You? (with Greg L. Hawkins)

Follow Me: What's Next for You? (with Greg L. Hawkins)

Focus: The Top Ten Things People Want and Need from You and Your Church (with Greg L. Hawkins)

Move: What 1,000 Churches Reveal About Spiritual Growth (with Greg L. Hawkins)

To pastors everywhere—
with gratitude for their passion, courage, and commitment
to serving as the shepherds of our souls

CONTENTS

THE HOPE OF *RISE*

The world is round.

The greatest discoveries aren't always life-changing inventions like the lightbulb or penicillin. Rather, the most significant game changers are often the recognition of realities that change the way we think. Like the discovery that the world is not flat, which set the stage for exploration that transformed human history.

In 2004, in its very first survey, REVEAL found this unexpected reality:

Church activities do not produce spiritual growth.

More specifically, increased participation in church activities does not significantly contribute to an increasing love of God and others.

This hallmark discovery challenged and eventually changed the mind-set of thousands of church leaders. Today its truth is confirmed by hundreds of surveys done over the last decade—with churches ranging from Pentecostal to Presbyterian; from those with weekend attendance of fifty to those with five thousand; from inner-city storefront locations to sprawling suburban campuses. The counterintuitive nature of this discovery prompted an exhaustive search for the answer to this question: What can churches do to become more effective change-agents for Christ?

Rise provides that answer, grounded in findings from its unmatched dataset on the spiritual lives of hundreds of thousands of churchgoers and enhanced by the first-person accounts of pastors and church leaders whose survey results have spurred successful spiritual growth initiatives. But more importantly, *Rise* opens with another mentality-changing discovery:

Churches are more similar than unique. Every church falls into one of eight patterns of spiritual growth effectiveness.

Rise reveals eight defining archetypes, and every church fits one of them—including yours. Those archetypes vary widely, from the Troubled Church introduced in chapter 2 to the Vibrant Church described in chapter 9. And each archetype has a different answer to the question "What's our next step toward becoming more effective for Christ?"

Rise will take you on an illuminating journey through the dynamics of eight distinct church cultures—a journey with the potential to forever change how you lead your church.

CHAPTER 1

THE THINGS REVEALED

The secret things belong to the LORD our God, but the things
revealed belong to us and to our children forever.

DEUTERONOMY 29:29

We thought we were done.

Not with the work. We knew that was far from finished. The number of REVEAL church clients was growing, along with the demands of processing surveys and generating reports. But we thought that the discovery phase was behind us—that the most dramatic insights about spiritual growth had been revealed and were, in fact, already built into the survey.

We were wrong.

It was 2009, and by then, nearly eight hundred churches had their eagerly awaited REVEAL survey results in hand. *But what are we supposed to do with them?* pastors asked. Although we had tried our best to make the reports and their numbers self-explanatory, they were still filled with statistics that many found confusing.

So they called. They asked questions. And together we discussed individual survey reports, working to arrive at a few takeaways that would benefit their ministry.

Then, after about fifty such consultations, it happened. Not a burning bush or a lightning bolt. Just one consultation that seemed almost identical to a handful of earlier ones—and soon, additional patterns of undeniable similarities began to surface from otherwise independent conversations.

As those similarities mounted, the REVEAL team sensed the prospect of a truly powerful discovery: Was it possible, we wondered, to determine if these patterns could be verified statistically as viable, replicable profiles? Could such profiles define America's church culture in conclusive, concrete terms?

Rise reveals the extraordinary outcome from this quest—a powerful framework that, with precision and depth, identifies and clarifies eight church patterns, which we call "archetypes," that define church culture in the United States. The intuitive appeal of this framework allows pastors everywhere—regardless of church size, denomination, or geography—to recognize their church's likely profile, and then to unlock the wealth of knowledge that underlies their archetype. (Each of the eight archetypes are depicted in Chart 1.1 and described briefly in the following sidebar.)

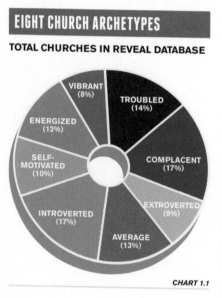

EIGHT CHURCH ARCHETYPES

TOTAL CHURCHES IN REVEAL DATABASE

VIBRANT (8%)
TROUBLED (14%)
ENERGIZED (12%)
SELF-MOTIVATED (10%)
COMPLACENT (17%)
INTROVERTED (17%)
EXTROVERTED (9%)
AVERAGE (13%)

CHART 1.1

Chapters 2 through 9 unpack these archetypes in depth, including fact-based descriptions, stories about churches that are classic examples of each archetype, and a case study that details how one church advanced from its original archetype position to another of greater spiritual impact.

First, though, chapter 1 will explain how the archetypes came

EIGHT CHURCH ARCHETYPES: A SNAPSHOT

1. THE TROUBLED CHURCH (14%)
  – People are spiritually immature and unhappy with the church and its senior pastor.

2. THE COMPLACENT CHURCH (17%)
  – Faith is surprisingly underdeveloped, given that attenders are longtime churchgoers.

3. THE EXTROVERTED CHURCH (9%)
  – Faith is underdeveloped, but community service is embraced.

4. THE AVERAGE CHURCH (13%)
  – No spiritual measures deviate from the norm.

5. THE INTROVERTED CHURCH (17%)
  – Faith is strong, but faith-based behaviors are lacking.

6. THE SELF-MOTIVATED CHURCH (10%)
  – Faith is strong across the board, yet people are unenthused about the church.

7. THE ENERGIZED CHURCH (12%)
  – Faith is somewhat underdeveloped but growing, and people love the church.

8. THE VIBRANT CHURCH (8%)
  – Faith is strong and mature but still growing, and people love the church.

SIDEBAR

together, an explanation that starts with a brief tour of the two primary buckets of REVEAL findings uncovered over the last ten years.

BUCKET #1: THE PEOPLE FACTOR

The starting point, and the foundation for all REVEAL discoveries including the archetypes, is the Spiritual Continuum (see Chart 1.2). In essence, the Continuum defines four stages of spiritual growth based on how a person describes his or her relationship with Christ.

These stages of spiritual growth are covered extensively in prior REVEAL books, notably, *Move: What 1,000 Churches Reveal About Spiritual Growth*. The most important takeaway for readers of *Rise* is that these four stages are powerful, consistent predictors of all factors related to spiritual growth measured by REVEAL. In other words, as a person's relationship with Christ matures through these four stages, *everything rises*—from acceptance of the core Christian beliefs, like

THE SPIRITUAL CONTINUUM

TOTAL CONGREGANTS IN REVEAL DATABASE

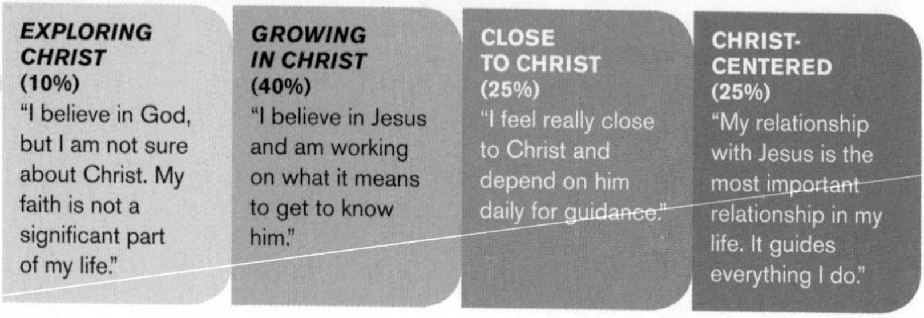

EXPLORING CHRIST (10%)	GROWING IN CHRIST (40%)	CLOSE TO CHRIST (25%)	CHRIST-CENTERED (25%)
"I believe in God, but I am not sure about Christ. My faith is not a significant part of my life."	"I believe in Jesus and am working on what it means to get to know him."	"I feel really close to Christ and depend on him daily for guidance."	"My relationship with Jesus is the most important relationship in my life. It guides everything I do."

CHART 1.2

belief in the Trinity, to how often a person prays or opens a Bible. Literally hundreds of factors related to spiritual growth increase exponentially as people advance from Exploring Christ to becoming Christ-Centered. This input was crucial to the creation of the archetypes because, of course, increased spiritual maturity is *exactly* what churches are trying to accomplish.

The most important input, however, was *not* the Continuum itself—but, rather, it was the discovery of *what helps people move* along the Continuum. Chart 1.3 illustrates three movements and the three core catalysts of spiritual growth.

THREE MOVEMENTS AND CATALYSTS OF SPIRITUAL GROWTH

✓ **MOVEMENT 1: BELIEFS**

✓ **MOVEMENT 3: FAITH IN ACTION**

EXPLORING CHRIST · GROWING IN CHRIST · CLOSE TO CHRIST · CHRIST-CENTERED

✓ **MOVEMENT 2: PERSONAL SPIRITUAL PRACTICES**

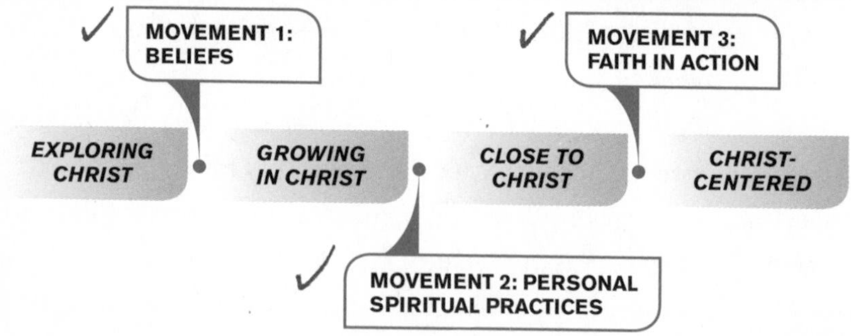

CHART 1.3

CORE CATALYSTS OF SPIRITUAL GROWTH

MOVEMENT 1: BELIEFS

Early spiritual growth is about building trust in the character of Jesus, so building a firm foundation of core Christian beliefs is essential. Catalysts include beliefs in:
>> Salvation by grace
>> The Trinity
>> A personal God
>> Authority of the Bible

MOVEMENT 2: PERSONAL SPIRITUAL PRACTICES

Intermediate spiritual growth is about developing a personal relationship with Christ, which depends on investing time to communicate with God. Catalysts include:
>> Reflection on Scripture
>> Prayer for guidance
>> Solitude

MOVEMENT 3: FAITH IN ACTION

Advanced spiritual growth is about surrendering everything to God, and dedicating significant time and energy to serve his purposes. Catalysts include:
>> Willingness to risk everything for Christ
>> Evangelism
>> Serving those in need

CHART 1.4

It became obvious that these three categories of catalysts would shed light on whether or not distinct patterns of discipleship effectiveness existed—because these are the things congregants must experience in order for spiritual growth to occur. Chart 1.4 summarizes the most significant catalysts for each movement.

This became the first big bucket of evidence to explore in the quest to identify the archetypes. It may seem that this could have been all the information that was necessary, since we had assembled the most influential "ingredients" for spiritual growth. But just as the ingredients for whatever you're making for dinner do not cook themselves by sitting untouched on the kitchen counter, a major component in our search for the archetypes was still missing. While in possession of hundreds of thousands of data points about the catalysts—the ingredients—of personal spiritual growth, we were still without the "recipe." So before any conclusions could be drawn, it was important to pull together everything we knew about the church.

BUCKET #2: THE CHURCH FACTOR

Even pastors who professed to enjoy statistics complained about having to wade through a forty-five-page REVEAL report to discover what their survey findings had to say about their church. "Net it out for me," they said. "Let me know where we stand on one page. Give it to me straight—short and sweet."

So the REVEAL team created the Spiritual Vitality Index (SVI). The SVI is a gauge that measures the spiritual maturity of a congregation and the discipleship effectiveness of its church. As illustrated in Chart 1.5, the SVI was intentionally designed to reflect the familiar academic grading scale—meaning that scores over 70 are above average and those under 70 are below average.

Like the Continuum, the SVI is useful, but static—in other words, it doesn't give pastors any practical insights about what can be done to increase the number. Its only objective was to satisfy the request of pastors for a spiritual vitality "snapshot"—and even

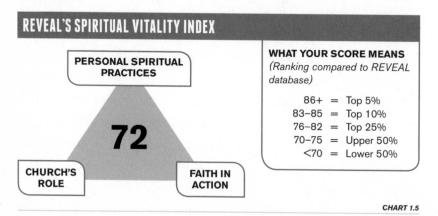

REVEAL'S SPIRITUAL VITALITY INDEX

PERSONAL SPIRITUAL PRACTICES

72

CHURCH'S ROLE

FAITH IN ACTION

WHAT YOUR SCORE MEANS
(Ranking compared to REVEAL database)

86+	=	Top 5%
83–85	=	Top 10%
76–82	=	Top 25%
70–75	=	Upper 50%
<70	=	Lower 50%

CHART 1.5

though they said they wanted it, not all REVEAL church leaders are thrilled to confront such a black-and-white, unambiguous assessment as soon as they open their report. "I've never been average at anything in my life!" is a common response from pastors facing an SVI in the 60s or 70s.

The SVI wound up playing an incredibly valuable role in the hunt for the archetypes. Like a Geiger counter that scours terrain in search of the most potent source of radioactivity, the SVI allowed us to comb through hundreds of reports to identify the churches achieving the highest marks. That search led to an in-depth study of sixteen churches—a study that yielded great fruit: the five best practices that advance spiritual growth, highlighted in Chart 1.6.

These five Best Practice Principles represent the church strategies that help pastors move their people along the Continuum because, according to all the REVEAL research done to date, churches must activate these strategies for discipleship to advance.

FIVE BEST PRACTICES THAT HELP CHURCHES ADVANCE SPIRITUAL GROWTH

GET PEOPLE MOVING
Jump-start newcomers with clear next steps by offering a spiritual "on-ramp" (like Alpha). Make the discipleship path and destination clear.

EMBED THE BIBLE IN EVERYTHING
Make Scripture the heart of the church culture. Take away people's excuses by doing whatever you can to make Bible engagement easy.

CREATE OWNERSHIP
Help people "own" the vision of the church. Use your small group system to empower and equip them to grow as leaders.

PASTOR THE LOCAL COMMUNITY
Make the local community your mission field by partnering with other churches and nonprofits to tackle local problems.

CHRIST-CENTERED LEADERSHIP
Surrender all leadership dilemmas and decisions to Christ. Humility and transparency are key.

CHART 1.6

Returning to our earlier analogy, if the catalysts (Chart 1.4) are the "ingredients" for spiritual growth, the five best practices provide the "recipe"—the instructions—for what the church needs to do in order to allow the "heat" of the Holy Spirit to create spiritual momentum.

Together, the Spiritual Growth Catalysts and the Best Practice

Principles served up a wealth of evidence to explore and analyze as we began a serious, intentional hunt for the archetypes.

THE BREAKTHROUGH

God lit our path in this search, providing insight once again through our one-on-one consultations with REVEAL client pastors. These conversations allowed us to create hypotheses—theories regarding which archetypes might emerge. For example, we talked with a number of very dissimilar congregations in terms of size, theology, and demographics that shared the *same* low spiritual beliefs, the *same* lukewarm relationship between congregants and the church, the *same* long-term tenure of church attendance, and the *same* minimal personal spiritual practices. These similarities prompted the search for an archetype now known as the Complacent Church.

More patterns surfaced. The Troubled Church was obvious, with its high dissatisfaction rates. The Introverted Church was also easy to spot, with above-average dedication to spiritual beliefs and practices but well-below-average expression of faith outside of its tight church circle of believers. These and additional patterns emerged out of pure conjecture, based on conversations with pastors leading churches with surprisingly similar survey results. Then—with the mountain of evidence narrowed by a dozen possible archetype pathways—we went to work to find whatever God wanted to reveal. Chart 1.7 brings the final outcome to life.

Merging the Best Practice Principles and the Spiritual Growth Catalysts produced a clear portrait of eight individual archetypes, each one with distinct strengths and weaknesses.[1] For example, in the upper right quadrant the Self-Motivated Church represents a congregation that has strong spiritual maturity but is unimpressed with its

---

[1] For a more detailed description of the statistical methodology used to develop the archetypes, see Appendix.

THE ARCHETYPES EMERGED

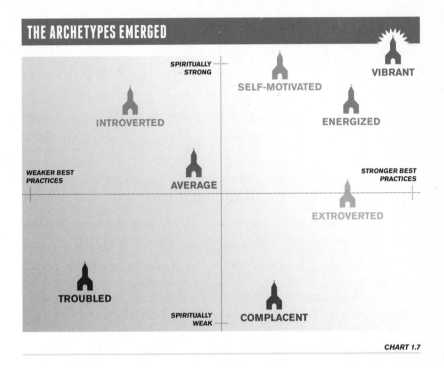

CHART 1.7

church. On the other hand, the Extroverted Church in the lower right quadrant is fully engaged and on board with everything its church is doing, despite the fact that its spiritual maturity is lacking.

What does all this mean? In the past, the path to becoming a spiritually "vibrant" church has been elusive, mysterious, even unknown. Today that path can be understood and pursued—particularly if a church knows its starting point. For instance, Chart 1.7 visually demonstrates that a Troubled Church has <u>much more ground to cover than an Average Church</u>, and a Complacent Church has a different path to "vibrancy" compared to an Introverted Church, which should pursue very different strategies than an Energized Church. The rest of this book is dedicated to describing *everything* REVEAL has uncovered about these eight archetypes—including, most importantly, what we know about the path to greater spiritual impact regardless of a church's current archetype position.

+ + +

Through these archetypes, we believe—as Moses wrote in Deuteronomy—that God has made known more "things revealed." Moses, of course, was writing about the law. But the spirit of his words transcends the millennia, we think, to remind us that God holds us accountable—not for the "secret things" known only to him, but for those things he decides to reveal.

REVEAL was accountable for pursuing the doors God opened to find these archetypes. We were also accountable for communicating them to you, a responsibility we consider to be a privilege. It is our prayer and greatest hope that you, too, will feel accountable—for learning about, and ultimately acting upon, these remarkable "things revealed."

TROUBLED

COMPLACENT

EXTROVERTED

AVERAGE

INTROVERTED

SELF-MOTIVATED

ENERGIZED

VIBRANT

CHAPTER 2

THE TROUBLED CHURCH

"Do you ever see churches where people just grade lower?"

Denial. That's the first reaction of most Troubled Church pastors to the high dissatisfaction and shallow spirituality found in their REVEAL reports. Although they often try to explain away the results by asking questions like the one above, most also acknowledge they suspected that an undercurrent of unhappiness existed and might be spreading among their congregants. Sometimes they confide that this is why they encouraged their church to take the survey—to find out what was up.

But to discover their church dissatisfaction is double the REVEAL norm (which it frequently is) and to find that dissatisfaction with the senior pastor runs even higher (which is commonly the case)—that can be a personal and spiritual blow. Like consulting a physician about an annoying ache or pain, only to learn the diagnosis is much more grim.

When the denial—and shock—wear off, two responses are classic.

One of these is isolation, sometimes brought to light when the church staff calls REVEAL to inquire about the delay in receiving their report. (Since survey results are distributed exclusively to the senior pastor, this means either the report is lost in the church's spam filter or the senior pastor is sitting on the findings.) The second response, one of stepping up to reality, is, thankfully, more common—mirroring Vince Lombardi's famous quote, "It's not whether you get knocked down, it's whether you get up."

Many Troubled Church pastors do exactly that—they pick themselves up, dust off the disappointment, and step out of denial into action. A great example is the senior pastor of a five-hundred-person church in the Northeast who, while driving to a church leader retreat, frantically called the REVEAL team, pleading to talk to *anyone* about his survey results. Immediately!

His report showed that his congregation was very unhappy with the church and that spiritually, they were coasting—a classic Troubled pattern. The pastor was choked up but determined. "I've been the pastor here for twelve years, and I know these people," he said. "We can do a better job. I *know* we can. That's what this retreat is all about. We're going to shake things up!"

Shaking things up is just what the doctor ordered for Troubled Churches—which are marked first and foremost by high dissatisfaction with the church and its leaders. Sources of the dissatisfaction range widely. Often a highly visible staff leader, like a teaching pastor or worship director, has resigned. Or a change in location has had a detrimental impact. For example, a Troubled Church in Michigan had moved from a small blue-collar town to the outskirts of Ann Arbor, and the mix of veteran churchgoers with the University of Michigan's student population was not going well. Interestingly, the move had occurred *five years* before their REVEAL survey—but the congregants' unhappiness was still evident.

Their story illustrates a disturbing but unsurprising truth about this archetype—that the roots of its distress tend to be long-standing, run very deep, and almost certainly will be difficult to unearth. While nothing is impossible with the Holy Spirit engaged in the battle, the Troubled Church tests the souls and convictions of its leaders like no other archetype.

Another Troubled Church, this one in Jackson, Mississippi, provides an additional window on the difficulties these churches may confront. Hurricane Katrina crushed Mississippi in 2005, and Jackson, as its state capital, is still dealing with the aftermath of this devastating storm. So are its churches.

Founded in the 1950s, this Troubled Church continues to step up to the lingering challenges from Katrina. For example, one-third of its congregants participate every month with recovery efforts, often through a coalition of churches that supports a food pantry, halfway houses, and other community services. But the church also struggles with issues related to racial tension aggravated by Katrina, and it wrestles with its direction, especially given the recent departure of its senior minister.

Unfortunately, these pressures are putting stress on a relatively weak spiritual foundation. Satisfaction with the church is only 34 percent, well below the 50 percent REVEAL norm. More importantly, a somewhat superficial spirituality seems to mark its culture. Core Christian beliefs are well below average, and personal spiritual practices, such as daily prayer and reflection on Scripture, are also subpar.

Many (almost one of five) say their spiritual growth is "stalled." Arguably, one could apply that description to the church as a whole. So when Katrina blew through its community, there was little of substance to withstand the spiritual crisis in its wake.

The storms that create Troubled Churches come in many shapes and sizes. As mentioned, it could be an unpopular change in location or an unexpected staff transition. It might be a community suddenly

TROUBLED
COMPLACENT
EXTROVERTED
AVERAGE
INTROVERTED
SELF-MOTIVATED
ENERGIZED
VIBRANT

caught in the vise of unemployment or battle lines drawn between advocates of traditional versus contemporary music. But something happens that shakes the church's spiritual core, and the weakness of that core has the potential to sink its future.

Pastors of the REVEAL Troubled Churches should be admired for their courage. Their decision to take the survey meant they were not only asking for a spiritual "report card" on the church and its leaders—they were also going public about their desire for congregational feedback, creating expectations that they would take action as a result. Given that most were aware that problems were likely to be exposed, this was "high stakes" leadership.

That kind of courageous, "rock the boat" leadership is mandatory for a Troubled Church turnaround—because getting the facts is only the beginning of a long, arduous journey. Once the facts are in hand, Troubled Church leaders need to move beyond the natural knee-jerk reaction of denial (or even anger) related to circumstances that may seem overwhelming. The best way to do that is to lean into Scripture, which proves time and again that nothing is impossible when God is in your corner.

"Be strong and courageous! Do not be afraid or discouraged. For the LORD your God is with you wherever you go" (Joshua 1:9, NLT). Troubled Churches need to embrace God's message to Joshua. Be strong and courageous—because a turnaround, a victory over whatever obstacles are in the way, can be yours.

SIX FACTORS THAT SET THE TROUBLED CHURCH APART

1. Spiritually Shallow

Congregants of Troubled Churches have low levels of beliefs, show little engagement in personal spiritual practices, and are not doing much to put their faith into action (see Chart 2.1). Nearly 60 percent of congregants in Troubled Churches are in the first two stages of the

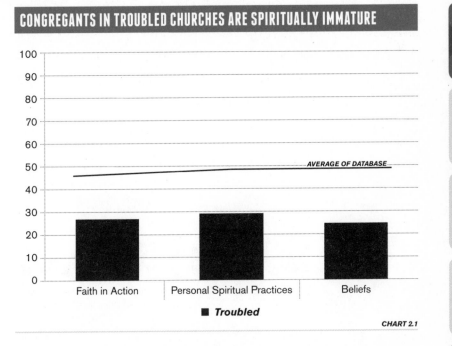

CONGREGANTS IN TROUBLED CHURCHES ARE SPIRITUALLY IMMATURE

AVERAGE OF DATABASE

Faith in Action | Personal Spiritual Practices | Beliefs

■ *Troubled*

CHART 2.1

spiritual continuum (see Chart 1.2), despite being longtime church attenders. Based on previous REVEAL research, it is unlikely that those who remain in the Exploring Christ stage of growth despite long tenures of church attendance will ultimately choose to follow Christ. In short, congregants in Troubled Churches are stuck, and they need more direction and support from their church to get their spiritual journeys in gear.

2. Pervasive Unhappiness

Extreme unhappiness about pretty much every aspect of church life characterizes congregants in Troubled Churches. They give the lowest ratings of any archetype for their satisfaction with the church's role in their spiritual growth and with the Best Practice Principles (see Chart 1.6). These ratings aren't just slightly lower—they are in the basement. Satisfaction with the senior pastor is at 28 percent, which is 15 percentage points below the average of all churches in

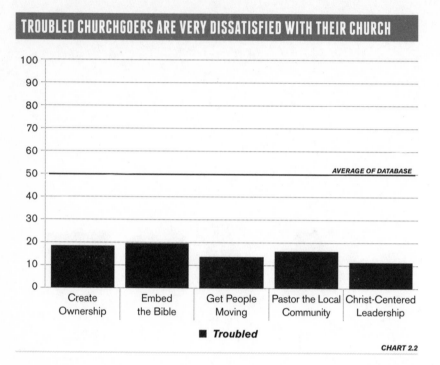

TROUBLED CHURCHGOERS ARE VERY DISSATISFIED WITH THEIR CHURCH

CHART 2.2

the REVEAL database. Less than 9 percent of congregants are highly satisfied with how the church is helping them grow, compared to an average of 16 percent across all churches. Chart 2.2 shows how Troubled Churches compare to the average in their satisfaction with the Best Practice Principles.

3. Unfocused Leaders

Given the high dissatisfaction among Troubled Church congregants, it is interesting to note what is—or is not—the self-reported focus of the leaders of Troubled Churches. When asked about the extent to which their church helps congregants develop a personal relationship with Christ, challenges them to grow, helps them understand the Bible, and inspires them to take ownership of the church and of their spiritual journeys, 6 percent or less of Troubled Church leaders very strongly agreed that any of these positive actions characterized their church. (By comparison, in a Vibrant Church very strong agreement with these statements averages 20 to 30 percent.) The only statement that garnered more than 10 percent agreement among Troubled Church leaders was "We help congregants in their time of emotional need"—a characteristic that, while important, is not particularly catalytic to spiritual growth.

4. Shrinking Congregation

Given the high levels of dissatisfaction in the congregation, it isn't surprising that the Troubled Church is more likely than all other archetypes to represent a smaller congregation (under 250) and to report declining attendance. Nearly half of Troubled Churches say their attendance has declined over the past year. They also have the lowest average adult weekend worship attendance of any archetype.

5. Conventional Culture

Troubled Church leaders are much more likely than those leading any other archetype to choose *traditional* or *mainline* as the best one-word description of their church. No Troubled Churches describe themselves as seeker-targeted, progressive, or fundamentalist. More than 25 percent of Troubled Churches say that their church's signature program is operating a Christian preschool—not exactly the core mission of a thriving church. Leaders of Troubled Churches are less likely than others to say that more catalytic programs such as offering a structured plan for spiritual growth, recovery groups, or small groups are among their church's distinctives.

6. Mature, Well-Heeled Demographics

Troubled Churches tend to have congregants who are older, well-educated, and longtime churchgoers. On average, half of Troubled Church congregants are over the age of fifty, and more than 40 percent have attended the church for ten years or longer. Troubled Churches

TROUBLED

COMPLACENT

EXTROVERTED

AVERAGE

INTROVERTED

SELF-MOTIVATED

ENERGIZED

VIBRANT

tend to have a well-educated congregation, with more than 60 percent having earned college degrees. However, Troubled Church congregations do not differ from those of other churches in their household income level or degree of racial/ethnic diversity. Compared to other archetypes, they are equally likely to be found in any region of the United States and in urban, suburban, or rural communities.

The Church of Osage Hills fits many but not all of these Troubled Church criteria. This may be because their case study begins as a new pastor arrives to pick up the pieces after a major fissure in the church. But a more noteworthy point is its shift to the Complacent Church archetype, the spiritual "cousin" of the Troubled Church that is featured in the next chapter. Both the Complacent and Troubled Church archetypes struggle with congregations marked by spiritual immaturity despite long histories of church attendance. But the Troubled Church, like the one in this case study, also struggles with a deficit of congregant goodwill—which makes a spiritual turnaround very difficult to attain.

A TROUBLED-TO-COMPLACENT CASE STUDY: THE CHURCH AT OSAGE HILLS, OSAGE BEACH, MISSOURI

Visit the Welcome page on The Church at Osage Hills website and you will find the following description: "Ken Lumley, our lead pastor, presents messages that are biblically based and sensitive to life's ups and downs." Certainly Ken and his church know all about ups and downs. It was the "downs," in fact, that brought them together.

Ken was burned out on ministry. Just done. His departure from the Jefferson City, Missouri, church he had pastored for seven years had been abrupt, the differences with his church's board hurtful and disillusioning. Now that Ken was unemployed, his bills were mounting. So in late 2007, when he got a call from an Osage Beach church on a Thursday asking if he could preach on Sunday, he said, "If you can just give me a hundred dollars, I'll come down and speak." The caller asked if Ken knew anything about what was going on at the church. "I said no—only that their pastor had resigned a few months back. They said, 'Perfect!'"

When Ken arrived that Sunday, one of his previous sermons in hand, he was surprised by the obvious tension. And by the fact that the former pastor, his wife, and their three teenagers were seated in the second row. "I was like, 'What are you doing here? I thought you were gone.' He said, 'Yeah, we're having some meetings about that.'" Ken proceeded to teach, focusing on the search-me-and-know-me request in Psalm 139.

Little did he know that this same Scripture had been referenced at a pre-service leaders' meeting . . . that the associate pastor would resign that very morning . . . that a scheduled congregational meeting would be quickly canceled . . . or that the former pastor, along with five families at the core of the congregation's lay leadership, would subsequently start a new church less than half a mile away.

The church where Ken spoke hired consultants to help them navigate their way through this trouble. The consultants' first recommendation was to hire an interim pastor—and then, at a later date, to hire a different person as the permanent pastor. Congregants were united in their response: "Let's get that search-me-and-know-me guy!"

Ken planned to serve as the interim and then move on, unconcerned that he was ineligible for the permanent position. "At that stage, I didn't want the job," he says. "I didn't even really want to be in ministry anymore. To be candid, the church was just emotionally, spiritually decimated. I came in and was pretty open about some of what I had recently been through. And that really resonated, because we all just needed to heal."

A month into Ken's new job, his father passed away. Grieving, he assumed—given his previous church's bureaucratic culture—that there would be no paid time off. "I had just got this job after months of being unemployed, and my dad had been ill but had taken this strong turn for the worse, and I needed to go to Des Moines to walk through this with my mom and brother. I'm thinking they're not going to pay me because I haven't worked for them long enough— that's the kind of rules I had been used to. And these people just looked at me like that was the dumbest thing they had ever heard."

As Ken ministered to his congregation, his congregation did the same for him. "It wasn't that we were just kind of bleeding on each other; it was that we were kind of healing each other," Ken explains. "And after my dad passed, I increasingly saw myself wanting to be here—to be here in the long term." In April 2008, the congregation bypassed the advice against permanently hiring the interim pastor, naming Ken as their senior pastor.

✦ ✦ ✦

Securing a new pastor, however, was only one of many challenges they faced. The truth about any Troubled Church, like Osage Hills, is that its turnaround depends *not* on new programs or ministry strategies, but on newly inspired leadership (and oftentimes, new leaders). So, before tackling the creation of a new vision and direction for the church, Ken made two key decisions.

Leadership Decision #1 was to find new leaders for children, youth, and worship.

Faced with the necessity to redefine their church, most pastors might begin by revamping Sunday services and various programs for adults. But Ken passionately proposed to fix the children's ministry first, then to follow up with a fresh start in student ministries before investing in the spiritual formation of Osage Hills' adults. He estimated that the process would take about two years.

As he explained to his new congregation, Ken had, years earlier, become convinced by George Barna's now well-known research that an individual's worldview is basically in place by the age of thirteen. And that there is surprisingly little change in worldview—including matters of faith—after that age. "I get really amped up about kids," Ken admits. "In budget crunches, the last person to go will be my children's person. And the first hire from here until I'm dead will be my children's person."

True to his word, within a month after joining the church, Ken offered the role of full-time children's ministry director to a congregation member, a dynamic woman who has, according to Ken, "just done a nails job." (That's high praise.) Then it was time to turn the church's attention to student ministries—but first, there would be a slight detour, necessitated by the departure of the church's worship leader in June 2008.

Inspired by their progress in the children's ministry, Osage Hills went looking for the right worship leader for their "new" church. And once again the church was blessed with finding a talented and dedicated person, of whom Ken says, "He was, and has been, and remains dynamite. He's a great guy; a great talent." (Or in Ken-speak, "nails.")

With that role filled, it was back to looking for a student ministries director—specifically for sixth, seventh, and eighth graders. This search, however, required no effort. "After several months of mission work in Africa, Scott had come back to central Missouri to figure out what to do next," Ken explains. "He literally showed up at our door." At first, the church hired him as a part-time interim student leader, but once again the interim position became a full-time permanent one. Since Scott became its leader, Osage Hills' student ministry has grown from about a dozen kids to more than two hundred.

Leadership Decision #2 was to use REVEAL to evaluate their spiritual progress.

In September 2009, with key staff members in place and its

TROUBLED

COMPLACENT

EXTROVERTED

AVERAGE

INTROVERTED

SELF-MOTIVATED

ENERGIZED

VIBRANT

relaunch underway, Osage Hills opted to take the REVEAL survey. Feeling that the church had made progress in the past year, Ken says, "At this point, we were looking for something that could serve as kind of a benchmark." An above-average 38 percent of the congregation responded to the survey, with many individuals expressing appreciation at being asked to consider and share their personal evaluations. "We got so many powerful and positive reports," Ken says. "People just saying, 'That's not only good for the church, that was great for me.'"

But the church's five staff members, attending a retreat timed to coincide with the arrival of the survey results, felt less than great. That experience, Ken admits, was "jolting. We hadn't expected to put the ball out of the park, but we were hoping to get it a little more out of the infield." While some results were encouraging (satisfaction with the senior pastor, for instance, was at 69 percent), others were sobering. Those included satisfaction with the church's role in spiritual growth at a very low 25 percent and daily Bible reading at only 6 percent.

"It was hard," Ken says. "But you know, we had good people here, and everybody just kind of leaned in." The team left their retreat unified behind three goals:

1. To increase the church's interaction with the Bible;
2. To initiate activities that would foster relational connectedness among congregation members; and
3. To find ways to do both of these things in light of the obstacles created by their church's geography.

Located amidst the meandering tentacles of Lake of the Ozarks (a lake with more miles of shoreline than the Atlantic from Maine to Florida), the church coexists with each summer's half-million party-hungry visitors. For Osage Hills attenders, already dispersed throughout a very widespread area, this Memorial Day to Labor Day influx creates either long work hours or the incentive to pack up and leave for the summer. "So it becomes very challenging to find ministry models that we can sort of borrow from or play upon," explains Ken. "During the summer, we scale our schedule way back. We don't even have Wednesday nights for teenagers—because our kids just wouldn't show."

Osage Hills Embedded the Bible—by Challenging the Summer "Slump"

Osage Hills tackled their three goals by launching The Summer Challenge, a season-long combination of Bible reading and physical workouts that culminated in August with a 5K run. "We encouraged everyone to read through the New Testament, and we encouraged them to do some sort of physical exercise," Ken explains. "We told them, 'While you guys are traveling, out of town, on vacation, go. Have a great time. We love you. And while you're gone, let's be reading the Bible together and let's be working out.'"

Participants signed commitment cards that were hung from the lobby ceiling. They focused on 1 Timothy 4:7-8. The church provided seventy-five-day study guides, basing Sunday sermons on each week's readings. And they passed out T-shirts that said *The Summer Challenge: I'm In. Are You?* "Hundreds and hundreds of people around the lake, some of them not even part of our church, were wearing those T-shirts." Ken laughs. "The message was clear: You can be part of what we're doing here while you're still doing what you're doing there." Then everyone came back together in August, having read their Scripture, eager to interact with their fellow congregants and ready to run their race.

That success was followed by additional Scripture-reading incentives and Bible-based sermon series. Notable among them was an eleven-week series on forgiveness, preached before a graffiti-decorated mural illustrating the Chris Tomlin song, "No Chains on Me." A chain-link fence standing before the mural included a huge

TROUBLED

COMPLACENT

EXTROVERTED

AVERAGE

INTROVERTED

SELF-MOTIVATED

ENERGIZED

VIBRANT

lock—and the church distributed some two thousand small keys hung on strings. "We encouraged everyone to take a key and to wear it around their neck for as long as any grudge or anger remained in their life," Ken says. "We told everyone that at any time—during any song, any point in the sermon, anything—if you are able to forgive, you should come up without prompting or permission to hang your key on the cross at the front of the room." In the weeks ahead, hundreds of people did exactly that. And now those keys reside in Ken's office, all precious reminders of what Ken considers "the greatest run—the most impacting, difficult run" in his twenty-two years of ministry.

+ + +

Compared to Ken's first sermon, delivered to what was then an angry, troubled congregation, such experiences have to feel amazing. But would Osage Hills' follow-up REVEAL survey validate such a positive reaction? Yes indeed. Congregant satisfaction with weekend services increased from 61 to 82 percent. Both overall attendance and attendance frequency have also increased, as has satisfaction with the senior pastor (to 84 percent) and congregant gains in spiritual maturity. (The Growing in Christ segment, for example, represented 43 percent of the congregation in the first survey. But by the second survey, that number had dropped—and the two more mature categories, Close to Christ and Christ-Centered, had increased in a statistically meaningful way.)

What next? Well, during the summer of 2012, another staff person was hired. And yes, this one oversees spiritual formation and focuses on . . . adults! The overall relaunch strategy has taken somewhat longer than the two years predicted at its outset, but it has been extraordinarily effective. "The church has had sort of the emotional and spiritual—and I might even say the organizational—maturity to let the process unfold," Ken says. "It's been a really good run."

THE HOPE FOR THE TROUBLED CHURCH

Turnarounds are the stuff of legend. Take the story of born-in-the-garage Apple that stormed into the market with its Macintosh computer in the early '80s, then stalled and ditched cofounder Steve Jobs. Apple expanded, then stalled again—and then reinstated Jobs, who made the company a Wall Street rock star. Then there's the Boston Red Sox, who posted sixty-nine wins and ninety-three losses in 2012—then flipped that record to ninety-seven wins and sixty-five losses the very next year, capping the most spectacular turnaround in baseball history with a World Series championship. Stories like these capture our imagination.

"Turnaround" means a complete reversal of circumstances, and the hope for the Troubled Church is found within that word. To be specific, before Apple asked Jobs to return, and before the Red Sox began spring training in 2013—a key "turn" had taken place. Notwithstanding the damage to pride and reputation (and there was plenty of that in both stories), leaders had decided to bite the bullet and do whatever needed to be done to turn their respective ships around.

A Troubled Church needs to make that same "turn"—which means to decide, regardless of the damage done to egos or the effort required, to do whatever it takes to reverse its downward spiral. That decision may be much harder than the turn itself—for two reasons. The first relates to the lack of a systematic external gauge that creates the urgency necessary for a course correction. Granted, churches are well aware of their trends in attendance and tithing. But that's vastly different from watching the stock market ticker tape while sparring regularly with analysts and shareholders about decisions and direction—or the pressure for performance kept alive by 24-7 media outlets dissecting box scores and every nuance of success or failure.

Spared from that kind of public performance scrutiny, churches lack this unpleasant but effective accountability "mirror" that creates

TROUBLED
COMPLACENT
EXTROVERTED
AVERAGE
INTROVERTED
SELF-MOTIVATED
ENERGIZED
VIBRANT

Symptoms of a Troubled Church

A church likely falls into the Troubled Church archetype if these three primary characteristics exist:

1. *Congregants are spiritually coasting.* Pastors are aware that their congregants' foundation of faith is shaky—that their conviction with core beliefs is weak, their personal spiritual practices are minimal, and their faith is defined by habitual church attendance.
2. *Congregant concern and discontent with church leadership infuse the culture.* Complaints about trivial issues are on the rise, and pastors sense that a congregational undercurrent of frustration with church decisions and direction is gaining momentum.
3. *Church attendance is in decline, possibly in free fall.* Very few newcomers visit the church, and the attrition of veteran congregants is obvious.

urgency and inspires change. This contributes to the second reason it is so hard for churches to make the turn: the temptation to tweak. In other words, when internal measures deteriorate, pastors are inclined to fine-tune their existing ministry rather than make the radical choices necessary to affect a turnaround. As noted earlier, those choices are painful—so if pain can be postponed or dodged altogether, that's the road pastors will likely take. Sometimes until it's too late.

However, if a church does make the decision to turn, a wide range of turnaround stories (including REVEAL churches) indicate that the steps of the "how," though incredibly demanding, are surprisingly straightforward.

The first such step is a ruthless evaluation of leadership, which results in cutting and/or adding people to ensure that *only* those capable of reviving and redirecting the church are on board. In *Good to Great,* Jim Collins described this step as making sure "the right people are on the bus."[1] Step two includes bringing renewed and relentless focus to the mission, frequently going back to the "basics"—which means returning to the fundamentals of the Great Commission. Once focus is restored, step three requires the removal of all distractions and obstacles in the church's path. This often requires the elimination of noncore activities, including long-standing but ineffective ministries.

The hope for the Troubled Church is that when the "turn" is made—meaning that leadership is recalibrated, mission is refocused, and distractions are removed—spiritual momentum will almost certainly accelerate. Eighty percent of all Troubled Churches that have taken the REVEAL survey more than once have changed archetypes. Most shift, at least initially, to the Complacent Church archetype, so they still have a great deal of work ahead. But to their credit and the glory of God, they have eradicated the troubled roots from the soul of their church.

In his first letter to the troubled church in Corinth, the apostle Paul echoed God's words in Joshua 1:9: "Stand firm in the faith. Be courageous. Be strong" (1 Corinthians 16:13, NLT). What magnificent counsel for Troubled Churches!

Stand firm: *No denial.*

Be courageous: *No isolation.*

Be strong: *No tweaking.*

Make the "turn" toward victory . . . for your church and for Jesus.

THE CHURCH OF OSAGE HILLS: 2014 UPDATE

What's the single biggest difference in the Church of Osage Hills since the case study?

Lead pastor Ken Lumley says that the most significant difference is the increased energy devoted to creating community impact. The

---

[1] Jim Collins, *Good to Great* (New York: HarperCollins, 2001), 13.

TROUBLED

COMPLACENT

EXTROVERTED

AVERAGE

INTROVERTED

SELF-MOTIVATED

ENERGIZED

VIBRANT

church tried to generate traction through a traditional home-based small group strategy. But due to its resort setting and widespread distances between homes, that was a struggle. So Ken decided, instead, to use community-service projects to draw people in for connection and assimilation. Today the church partners with six school districts to provide Buddy Packs, packages of food items provided to low-income children for weekend nutrition. Ken says hundreds of people show up every week to create these gifts for the schools, which he describes as an intentional step toward becoming a redemptive agent in the community.

What's new in the church's discipleship strategies and culture since the case study?

Two strategies have advanced discipleship, including a reprise of the successful Summer Challenge, this year focused on encouraging congregants to engage with Psalms and Proverbs during the hyperactive summer season. In addition, Ken has used his teaching to more directly unpack the "nature of the Kingdom in the present," bringing attention to God's presence in the midst of life's messiness—a message that Ken says has been very popular with the congregation.

What's next on the horizon for the Church of Osage Hills?

Ken sees continued forward momentum from the "tremendous response" to their community service focus. In fact, the church budget recently allocated a significant investment to broaden and deepen its community impact.

CHAPTER 3

THE COMPLACENT CHURCH

TROUBLED

COMPLACENT

EXTROVERTED

AVERAGE

INTROVERTED

SELF-MOTIVATED

ENERGIZED

VIBRANT

Remember the boiling frog story?

This popular anecdote places a comfortable, happy frog in a kettle of tepid water atop an open flame. As the water temperature gradually heats up, the frog remains unaware of the danger and falls into a tranquil stupor until disaster strikes.

The frog's problem is complacency—defined as "a feeling of quiet pleasure or security, often while unaware of some potential danger."[1] This describes the Complacent Church to a T. Because despite weekly reminders—often for many years—about the truth and power of the gospel, Complacent Church congregants are in a spiritual stupor, content with a faith characterized by a relatively superficial relationship with their church rather than a deepening relationship with Jesus. Many Complacent congregants are repeatedly tuning out the message that God has "plans to prosper you and not to harm you, plans to give you hope and a future" (Jeremiah 29:11). But weeks fade into years as the possibility of that abundant life passes them

---

[1] *Random House Dictionary*, s.v. "complacency."

by, and as advancing age tightens the noose around the promise of salvation and redemption.

Pastors are rarely surprised to hear that they lead a Complacent Church. Take the example of a large mainline church in Missouri. Their REVEAL survey report showed that congregants were life-long churchgoers who defined their spirituality almost exclusively by church activities. At best, their engagement with prayer and Scripture outside the church was minimal. And their conviction with core beliefs, like salvation by grace and authority of the Bible, was shockingly low. Interestingly—given the scant indications of any kind of spiritual depth—the number of people who described their spiritual growth as "stalled" was also quite low.

Their pastor was disappointed, but not surprised. "It's hard to know you're stalled," he said, "if you don't know there's a journey."

Such lack of awareness that they are, in fact, on a spiritual journey (albeit moving at a snail's pace) is one of several typical deficiencies found in Complacent Church congregations. A pastor serving in the Texas panhandle referenced another when he said with a sigh, "Sometimes I think I'm leading a social club instead of a church." His Complacent Church, an all-white congregation, was reluctant to diversify in step with its ethnically changing community. This reflects a common Complacent Church malady, which is the tendency for the church to become a place where congregants look forward to rubbing shoulders with like-minded people in their community—sadly, more than they look forward to an encounter with God. In fact, they likely don't even think that such a life-changing encounter is possible.

Another issue compounding this spiritual quagmire is that the roots of complacency run deep. Many Complacent Church congregants have attended their church for more than a decade. REVEAL statistics show this longevity becomes a detriment to spiritual progress at the five-year mark, which is when churchgoers who have yet to accept Christ become far less likely to do so.

Speaking of longevity, the pastor of a Complacent Church in Springfield, Illinois, laughed when asked how long the church had been in place. He said church lore claims Abraham Lincoln attended revivals at the church, which was founded in 1821. Maybe it wasn't complacent in the days of Honest Abe. But unfortunately, according to their REVEAL survey in November 2013, the temperature was unquestionably rising on this frog.

SEVEN FACTORS THAT SET THE COMPLACENT CHURCH APART

Seven factors, including but going beyond simple demographics, distinguish the Complacent Church:

1. On a Journey to Nowhere

About 60 percent of people attending Complacent Churches are in the first two stages of spiritual growth—Exploring or Growing in Christ—even though one-third of congregants have attended church for more than ten years. Complacent Church congregants report core Christian beliefs, personal spiritual practices, and faith-in-action behaviors that are at the very lowest levels of any church type, including Troubled Churches (see Chart 3.1).

2. Happy with the Status Quo

Unlike congregants in Troubled Churches, Complacent churchgoers seem to think their church is doing okay. They express fairly average satisfaction with their senior pastor and with the role the church plays in their spiritual growth. They are also generally appreciative of their church's efforts to live out most of the Best Practice Principles (see Chart 1.6). This acceptance of the "status quo" is what distinguishes Complacent from Troubled Churches.

3. Curious About Scripture

The one area of significant dissatisfaction in Complacent Churches is with the church's failure to "Embed the Bible" (see Chart 3.2). These

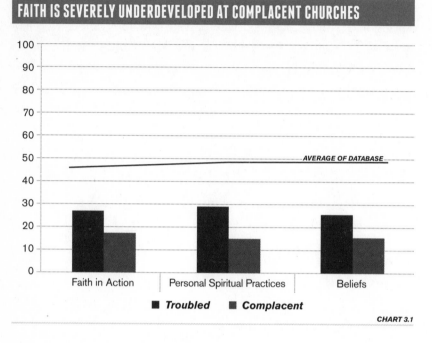

FAITH IS SEVERELY UNDERDEVELOPED AT COMPLACENT CHURCHES

CHART 3.1

congregants apparently want their church's help in understanding the Bible in greater depth, although that desire seems in direct contrast to their belief in the authority of Scripture, which is very low. So the lower satisfaction with "Embed the Bible" may indicate more of a curiosity about the spiritual context and content of Scripture than a real frustration with a lack of Bible-based teaching or support from the church. In any event, it definitely indicates an opportunity for Complacent Church pastors. The case study that follows this profile demonstrates what can happen when a Complacent Church recognizes and steps into this opening.

4. Growing in Numbers

More than half of all Complacent Churches report that their attendance has increased over the past twelve months, and about 30 percent report that their attendance is stable. These churches tend to be large,[2] with nearly 70 percent reporting an adult weekend worship attendance of 250 or more. This undoubtedly contributes to the frog-in-the-kettle phenomenon, because when attendance is stable or rising, it is more difficult for church leaders to notice the deeper, underlying problem of spiritual stagnation.

5. Traditional Denominations Seeking Seekers

Leaders of Complacent Churches tend to choose the words *mainline* and *seeker friendly* as the best descriptions of their church. The seeker-friendly descriptor may indicate a disconnect between these church leaders and their congregants, since less than 15 percent of Complacent Church congregants have spiritual conversations with their unchurched friends on a regular basis, and just 5 percent of them say they feel equipped to share their faith.

[2] Ninety percent of churches are under 250 in size, according to the 2012 National Congregations Study.

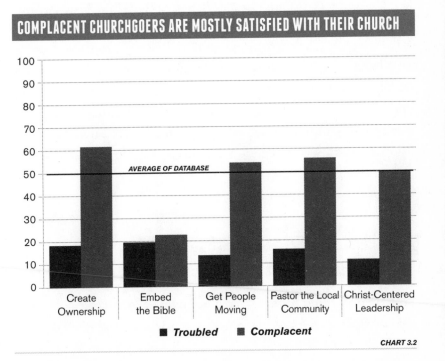

COMPLACENT CHURCHGOERS ARE MOSTLY SATISFIED WITH THEIR CHURCH

AVERAGE OF DATABASE

■ *Troubled* ■ *Complacent*

CHART 3.2

6. Focused on Worship Service Variety

When it comes to naming their church's signature programs, 40 percent of Complacent Church leaders choose offering multiple worship styles, far more than leaders of any other church type. Based on many conversations with Complacent Church pastors, a likely explanation is that they have expanded their service offerings to include both "contemporary" and "traditional" services. Congregant satisfaction with weekend worship services is slightly above average, indicating that the variety in styles resonates with them.

7. Wealthy, Well-Educated, Middle-America Suburbanites

A high percentage of Complacent Church congregants have college degrees and annual incomes of seventy-five thousand dollars or more. Nearly 80 percent of Complacent Churches are located in suburban communities, and about half are in the Midwest. Complacent Churches also tend to have little racial/ethnic diversity.

Nearly all of these seven characteristics were evident in the REVEAL survey results of the church described in the following case study. But thanks to the pastor you're about to meet, who was not content with "tweaking" the church's discipleship mission or strategy, this congregation banished its complacent spiritual temperament.

....

A COMPLACENT-TO-ENERGIZED CASE STUDY:
SOUTHWEST CHURCH OF CHRIST, JONESBORO, ARKANSAS

Preaching Minister Jimmy Adcox may have expected few, if any, surprises when his Southwest Church of Christ congregants took their initial REVEAL survey in January 2009. After all, during his thirty years at the Jonesboro, Arkansas, church, he'd witnessed the church's transition from its original conservative roots into the more progressive, grace-filled atmosphere it is known for today. He was well aware of the strong reputation the church enjoys in its university town of seventy thousand. And he may have assumed that the survey would reflect Southwest's heart for community service. (It did.)

What he didn't expect was that many of Southwest's nine hundred–plus people, including those who had faithfully attended and served for ten or even twenty years, remained in the earliest stages of spiritual growth. "That was kind of alarming," Jimmy admits. "I had thought of those in that first stage—Exploring Christ—as new people coming in, just looking at faith for the first time." But now it was clear that many longtime Southwest attenders were, for the most part, experiencing faith only in the context of church activities. Despite their long church tenure, their beliefs and attitudes were run-of-the-mill, and their Bible engagement behaviors were far below average. Jimmy remembers thinking, *They go to church, but they're really not living their lives as passionate disciples of Jesus.*

These initial results may have been somewhat less surprising to Southwest's attenders, given the fact that only 43 percent of them reported satisfaction with how the church was advancing their spiritual growth.[3] Like other Complacent Churches, what they said they needed most, in fact, was more help in "understanding the Bible in depth," a perceived deficiency that likely influenced one of every five survey takers to express dissatisfaction with their church.

But if the bad news was that the church had not been providing an optimal environment for fostering its people's spiritual maturity, the good news—actually, the *great* news—was that a significant majority of these people loved and respected their pastor. (While it is

---

[3] Southwest's below-average satisfaction contrasts with the more typical average church satisfaction in the classic Complacent Church profile. This illustrates how churches can vary a bit within an archetype, despite it being the best fit for their pattern of results.

TROUBLED
COMPLACENT
EXTROVERTED
AVERAGE
INTROVERTED
SELF-MOTIVATED
ENERGIZED
VIBRANT

not unusual for REVEAL survey results to show greater satisfaction with the pastor than with the church, Southwest's spread between the two was *double* what is typical.)

With that kind of credibility and trust—and the permission it implies—the stage was set for Jimmy and his team to lead Southwest's people on a vigorous, intentional spiritual-growth journey that hinged on two key leadership decisions and one timely leadership recalibration.

Leadership Decision #1 was to involve everyone in high-impact, focused initiatives.

Southwest's leaders were of one mind: Starting immediately, their church would move forward with purposeful, focused, intentional initiatives. "It wasn't a matter of saying, 'We want to encourage everybody to read their Bible,'" Jimmy shares. "Instead we planned a way to engage the church and do it *together*."

Leadership Decision #2 was to leverage renewed Bible immersion into ministry impact.

"From getting people in the Word to helping them move out beyond themselves into ministry and mission—that was a two-step movement that we became very intentional about," Jimmy explains. So they carefully selected the next sermon series, laying the groundwork to significantly expand outreach opportunities.

Southwest Embedded the Bible—by Tapping Outside Resources

In the past, Southwest had followed a typical path when selecting its Sunday sermon series: pick a topic, spend a few weeks exploring the various aspects of that topic, then move on to something else. Now, however, the mandate was clear. "We really wanted to get our people in the Word—consistently, over a long period of time," Jimmy says, so they tapped what they considered to be the ideal resource for that process: *The Story*, which had originated in San Antonio's Oak Hills Church by pastors Randy Frazee and Max Lucado.

This chronological journey through the Bible became a church-wide experience that involved not only Sunday services, but also the church's small groups, Bible classes, and even the children's ministry. "We went all out," Jimmy says. "We marketed it in the community; we got commitments from our people; we gave away books; we had people playing Bible characters on our launch Sunday. We really had a great time with it."

Beginning in the fall of 2009 and lasting for thirty-one weeks, Southwest's congregation read an average of fifteen pages of Scripture a week. Jimmy preached on that material each Sunday morning. Classes discussed it. "It was the buzz of conversation for about nine months," Jimmy says. "Even for those who had been long-term Christians, I think it was just a fresh reading of the Word, and they saw things they had never seen before. It helped tie together the whole message of Scripture."

Not only that, but attendance grew as people from Jonesboro and surrounding communities showed up to take part. "We found that there are people who are outside the church but who really want to know what the Bible is about," Jimmy says.

By the time they had completed *The Story*, Southwest's congregation was growing—in terms of both increased attendance and spiritual maturity. But neither leaders nor congregants counted their mission accomplished. Instead they looked for the best way— the most *intentional* way—to continue their immersion in the Bible while also beginning to ramp up the congregation's outreach into ministry and missions. This time, they decided to tap into Scot McKnight's *The Jesus Creed: Loving God, Loving Others.*

This new sermon series, which began in the fall of 2010, proved to be the ideal complement to the church's earlier study. Where *The Story* had spent much of its time in the Old Testament, *The Jesus*

TROUBLED

COMPLACENT

EXTROVERTED

AVERAGE

INTROVERTED

SELF-MOTIVATED

ENERGIZED

VIBRANT

Creed would focus on the Gospels. *The Story* had gotten Southwest's people into the Word, and *The Jesus Creed* not only built on that involvement but also inspired attenders' commitment to the needs of those outside the church. "It really did turn people outward," Jimmy says. "I mean, if you're going to follow Jesus, you're going to follow him out the door and into the world."

It was in the transition—from the launch of integrated Bible-based curriculum throughout the church, to an expanded outreach vision—that Southwest realized a recalibration was in order.

About halfway through *The Jesus Creed*, things began to feel "a little flat." Southwest met that concern head on, asking its church leaders to provide responses to four specific questions (What's right? What's wrong? What's confusing? What's missing?), as well as interviewing some sixty church families. "From the time we began that open conversation with the church, momentum began shifting," Jimmy says. "People kept talking about community." And church leaders began to sense that all of Southwest was trying to communicate: "We're tired of talking about it. Let's do it!"

Southwest Pastored the Local Community—with a Vision to "Overflow"

In response to its congregants' growing appetite for community impact, the church held its first Overflow Sunday, during which six hundred attenders spilled into the community after services, to partner with city officials as they assisted with forty-five different projects. (During a subsequent Overflow Sunday, congregants cleaned up several tons of trash from homes and yards, prompting Jonesboro's mayor to send the city's sanitation department on special pick-up runs!)

As further evidence of Southwest's passion, their capital campaign was modified to include funds to build a facility for the church's recently launched campus ministry at nearby Arkansas State University. (That facility, the "Wolf Life Center," opened in the fall of 2012.) Then the focus of Southwest's three-year, $2.2 million capital campaign expanded again, in response to the congregation's desire to pay off the church's debt in order to free up more cash to reach out to the community.

"Our people have grown in terms of being in the Word on their own," Jimmy says, "which in turn has impacted their spiritual life, which in turn has impacted their sense of mission and ministry."

Now Jimmy and his leadership team's challenges include timely follow-through and prayerful discernment, as they move toward opportunities that align with the passions and giftedness of Southwest's congregation. "There is this deep desire within our people for us to activate, together as a church, a more deliberate mission to reach our community," Jimmy explains. "But we don't want what we do to just be community service projects. We want our work to also include a focus on planting new communities of faith."

As they work toward these ends, described as their Overflow Vision, Southwest keeps three challenges in front of its people. First shared in a handout entitled "How God's Blessings Can Overflow into Our Community Through Me," the vision encourages all attenders to offer themselves in three ways that will facilitate God's "overflow" into their community:

1. *Overflow Opportunity #1: By Serving My World.* "The question this asks is, 'How can I be God's presence in my current sphere of influence?'" Jimmy explains. "'How can I see myself as sent by God into my job; into my neighborhood; into my school?' We're already there, and God already has a mission for us. We just have to see ourselves as his representative in those places."

2. *Overflow Opportunity #2: By Serving Outside My World.* This vision principle challenges attenders to extend their influence to people they don't yet know. Southwest's congregants are encouraged to find someplace in the

community to serve—as a tutor in a school, for instance, as a volunteer at the hospital, or as a mentor at City Youth, a Jonesboro ministry for at-risk kids. "We're asking, 'Where in the community can you plug in to help be on a mission for God in the lives of people you would never know or meet any other way?" Jimmy says.

3. *Overflow Opportunity #3: By Serving Through My Southwest Family.* Southwest has long had a heart for its community, so there are many existing ministries within the church that already offer positive impact to their fellow citizens. "In which existing ministry will you serve to help our Overflow Vision become a reality?" church leaders ask.

The vision, introduced early in 2012 to a congregation that now numbers about 1,100 Sunday attenders, is taking place as Jimmy closes in on thirty-five years with Southwest. He looks forward to focusing on the church's Overflow Vision during the fall of 2013. Such focus, he believes, has also been influenced by Southwest's participation in REVEAL. "I feel like I'm preaching *toward* something now, instead of just preaching," he says. "My sermons have been a lot more Jesus-centered; a lot more focused around the Kingdom of God and the power of transformation."

Southwest Benchmarked Its Progress in 2011

The spiritual momentum Jimmy intuitively sensed in 2012 was already in evidence in March 2011, when Southwest did a follow-up REVEAL survey. Virtually all measures of spiritual vitality had advanced—most in statistically significant ways. For example, belief in a personal God soared from 59 to 74 percent. Belief in the Authority of the Bible increased from 51 to 62 percent. Categories across the board—from personal spiritual practices, to participation *and* satisfaction with serving those in need through the church, to satisfaction with weekend services—all experienced significant upward movement. Their Spiritual Vitality Index rose from 63 to 74. And what about their strong satisfaction with the senior pastor in the first survey? Even higher this time.

Although Jimmy mentions no plans to take yet a third REVEAL survey, it is easy to imagine that such an initiative might once again lead to a few surprises. Pleasant ones.

THE HOPE FOR THE COMPLACENT CHURCH

The Southwest Church of Christ case study illustrates the kind of spiritual traction seen in many Complacent Churches when pastors challenge their people to engage in Scripture—often launching biblical literacy initiatives and/or Bible-based campaigns to jump-start spiritual momentum.

At Southwest, Jimmy Adcox's efforts not only inspired his own congregants to accelerate their spiritual pace, but also attracted others in the Jonesboro community to check out what all the fuss was about. Similar success stories are reported by Complacent Churches in very different circumstances—for example, in a large 1,000+ nondenominational church in Wisconsin where the senior pastor spent nine months teaching Biblical literacy classes before launching a Bible-based weekend campaign. And then there's the story of the flagship Presbyterian church in Pittsburgh, where the pastor spent a month teaching on the REVEAL Spiritual Continuum before turning to a one-year deep-dive into the book of Romans. Like Southwest, both these churches shifted over a two- to three-year period, from the Complacent to the Energized archetype.

But this final story may be the most encouraging of all. Six Lutheran churches, ranging in size from one hundred to three hundred congregants, decided to launch the same Bible-based campaign and gauge the impact with REVEAL. They used Scripture Union's

TROUBLED

COMPLACENT

EXTROVERTED

AVERAGE

INTROVERTED

SELF-MOTIVATED

ENERGIZED

VIBRANT

Symptoms of a Complacent Church

A church likely falls into the Complacent Church archetype if these three primary characteristics are true:

1. *Congregants are on a spiritual journey to nowhere.* People rarely pray or reflect on Scripture outside of church settings. Beliefs are weak. Faith is defined by church activities, and it is not a primary value guiding life decisions.
2. *Congregants are longtime, older churchgoers.* Half of the congregation (or more) is over age fifty and has attended church for at least ten years. Many would say they have attended church regularly for most of their lives.
3. *Congregants are happy with the church and its leadership.* Church leaders perceive a relatively high level of satisfaction, sensing that people are comfortable with the church and its leaders. Complaints are typically for issues like the decibel level or style of music, or superficial items like temperature or traffic control that are related to weekend services.

E100 program to challenge their people to read five Bible stories every week for twenty weeks, and almost everyone stepped up. The obstacles were great—demonstrated by a story told by one of these churches about its decision to refresh its pew Bibles in support of the initiative. Upon examination, it was clear that the Bibles had never been opened. Pages were mashed together. The book spines were stiff. Obviously, reading the Bible was far from the norm for their congregants, even during Sunday services.

Two years later—among all six congregations—satisfaction with the churches had soared. Dissatisfaction and "likelihood to leave" had declined dramatically. Bible reading had doubled. The aggregate Spiritual Vitality Index had increased from 53 to 57—an improvement, but one that left substantial potential for more progress.

However, signs of spiritual growth were evident, as were anecdotal stories about rekindled spiritual energy. Attendance did not increase, but it did remain stable—which the pastors counted as a victory.

Complacent Churches abound in the Christian landscape. Their relatively high percentage in the REVEAL database (17 percent) suggests that thousands of churches fall into this archetype. It's a tough place to be. But these stories of measurable change offer hope—great hope—that every one of these churches can *rise* and become much more dynamic, productive agents for Christ. It's not easy. A Complacent Church is a difficult assignment. But when focused, committed leadership leans into the Holy Spirit, it can be done. Chapter 10 expands on these Bible engagement strategies and provides more practical next steps for the Complacent Church.

SOUTHWEST CHURCH OF CHRIST: 2014 UPDATE

What's the single biggest difference in Southwest Church since the case study?

Senior minister Jimmy Adcox reports that greater intentionality now characterizes church leadership and has also been embraced by the congregation. The best leadership example is a "very intense" strategic planning session led by the Kairos Church Planting Executive Director, Stan Granberg, in June 2013. In fall 2014, on the verge of retiring debt and ready to respond to the open doors God will provide, Southwest leaders have launched a new three-part vision to:

1. *Multiply*—locally and regionally through groups, on-site venues, multisites, and church plants;
2. *Engage the Community*—by generously living on mission every day; and
3. *Maximize Ministry*—by increasing involvement and focus on life transformation.

Congregant intentionality is evidenced by impressive sales of Sarah Young's daily devotional *Jesus Calling*, which Jimmy says has been "flying off the shelves."

What's new in Southwest's discipleship strategies and culture since the case study?

The "multiply" goal has advanced, with the integration of several weekend sermon series into the church's small group curriculum. In the fall of 2013, Southwest's number of small groups increased from twenty to one hundred and twenty for an eight-week campaign based on the ten-year anniversary of *The Purpose Driven Life*. That number declined but still remained high at seventy for a twelve-week spring series based on Randy Harris's *Living Jesus* curriculum, focused on the Sermon on the Mount. These integrated series "just work for us," says Jimmy. Another favorite series was "Kingdom Assignment," which gave congregants a specific challenge each week, such as "Serve One" (serve one need that crosses your path) and "Ask Five" (offer to pray for the needs of five people). Jimmy appreciated the personal initiative inspired by this series, based on material by Denny Bellesi. As part of the vision toward missional living and community engagement, the congregation is being challenged to practice Michael Frost's "The Five Habits of Highly Missional People: Taking the BELLS Challenge to Fulfill the Mission of God."

What's next on the horizon for Southwest Church?

The first step toward multiplication will be an on-site missional venue, built not around worship style but around missional practice to reach people the church is not currently reaching. The second will be a multisite service on campus at Arkansas State University. Jimmy is also setting the stage for a multigenerational vision by coteaching with a younger minister on staff.

THE EXTROVERTED CHURCH

"The driving force that sets us apart is what we do, not what we say."

So states IV (pronounced "Ivy") Marsh, senior pastor of Epic Church—a dynamic Extroverted Church that in 2012 counted two thousand of Decatur, Alabama's fifty-five thousand residents among its worshipers. Epic paints the classic picture of an Extroverted Church operating in high gear:

- Sunday services are held in a metal barn beside a gravel parking lot, located just off a dead-end street a block from Decatur's ghetto. "We want to put money into people, not buildings," IV explains.
- Instead of collecting a Christmas offering, Epic distributes thousands of dollars to congregants, asking them to make someone's Christmas brighter—unless they need it themselves.

- Attenders do "reverse car washes," paying people three dollars for the privilege of washing their cars. They also show up regularly at street corners to hand out cold water when it's hot—or hot coffee when it's cold.
- A "game changer," according to IV, was a tornado that ripped through Lawrence County in 2010. With power completely out, Epic distributed work gloves, saws, and Gatorade. They provided childcare. And they raised enough money to put thirty-six mobile homes on the ground—a week before FEMA arrived. "FEMA exists because the church doesn't do its job," says IV.

Such an unconventional serving vision characterizes many Extroverted Churches, as does Epic's history as a church plant born of humble beginnings. In fact, this remarkable church was almost DOA in 2007. Three months after IV moved to Decatur to help a friend plant Epic, that friend—the senior pastor—bailed, making IV the leader by default. The then-one-hundred-and-seventy attendance dropped to one hundred, then sixty-seven, and by week three Epic was back to its original launch team of thirty-five. In response, IV shared his vision for beyond-the-norm community service with eight staff members. Four walked out.

The roller-coaster world of church planting—which can swing from near-disaster to victory in a matter of weeks or months—is home base for a high percentage of Extroverted Churches. What sustains them is their steadfast dedication to making the world a better place in the name of Jesus, demonstrated by their above-average serving attitudes and behaviors. This dedication is a magnet for the altruistic desire to help others that touches so many hearts—and explains why Extroverted Churches attract people who might otherwise shun church life.

But therein also lies the weakness of the Extroverted Church.

Its focus on transforming its community may distract from transforming people into followers of Christ. While their congregants may be open-hearted and responsive to calls for help from soup kitchens, halfway houses, or after-school programs for low-income children, their embrace of core Christian beliefs is relatively weak and their personal investment in communicating with God through spiritual practices is haphazard. To be blunt, an Extroverted Church risks becoming more like a nonprofit service organization than the bride of Christ.

There is much to admire about Extroverted Churches. Extroversion—"being concerned primarily with things outside the self, with the external environment rather than with one's own thoughts and feelings"[1]—is not a bad thing. Extroverted Churches make a real difference in the lives of people in their communities who struggle with significant challenges. But the Great Commission does not call the church first and foremost to serve those in need. It calls the church to "go and make disciples of all nations, baptizing them in the name of the Father and of the Son and of the Holy Spirit" (Matthew 28:19).

Extroverted Churches are off to a great start. They're attracting people to church who might otherwise never darken its door, and their impact for the Kingdom is likely profound. As IV Marsh says, "Evangelism is a gift. Witnessing is not. Just show up, do good, and people will notice what you do, not what you say." This is reminiscent of the oft-quoted statement attributed to St. Francis: "Preach the gospel at all times; when necessary, use words," which arguably could be the mantra for the Extroverted Church. The caution for this admirable and selfless church archetype is to avoid devoting so much energy to "doing good" that growing a relationship with Jesus inadvertently becomes a secondary priority.

---

[1] *Random House Dictionary*, s.v. "extroversion."

SIX FACTORS THAT SET THE EXTROVERTED CHURCH APART

1. Seeker Central

Many Extroverted Churches are relatively new, with 35 percent of those in the REVEAL database having launched since 1990. New churches typically focus on reaching seekers—a focus that is bearing fruit in Extroverted Churches. About one in eight congregants in Extroverted Churches is in the Exploring Christ stage (see Chart 1.2)—people who are interested in learning more about a relationship with Christ but who haven't yet committed themselves to following Him. Unlike in Troubled and Complacent Churches (the only two archetypes with a higher percentage of Explorers), seekers in Extroverted Churches tend to be newcomers—individuals who likely are more open to making a decision for Christ than those who have been in church for many years.

2. More Martha than Mary

In Extroverted Churches, a large percentage of congregants engage in faith-in-action behaviors like serving and evangelism. On average, 53 percent serve those in need at least once a month, either through their church or on their own (a rate that is 10 percent above the average for all churches); 20 percent serve once a week or more on their own (12 percent above average), demonstrating a strong commitment to follow Jesus' example of servanthood. Sadly, making time to sit at Jesus' feet isn't as high a priority for these churchgoers. As illustrated in Chart 4.1, their engagement in spiritual practices lags behind their faith in action, and their adherence to core beliefs is even lower.

3. Built for Community Service

Given the high level of congregant engagement in serving, it is not surprising that a whopping 75 percent of Extroverted Church leaders, far more than any other church type, say that local community outreach is their church's signature program. They also are more likely than others to very strongly agree with the statements, "We promote

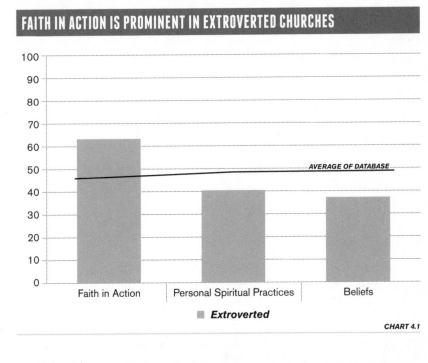

FAITH IN ACTION IS PROMINENT IN EXTROVERTED CHURCHES

AVERAGE OF DATABASE

Faith in Action | Personal Spiritual Practices | Beliefs

■ *Extroverted*

CHART 4.1

a strong serving culture that is widely recognized by the local community" and "We empower congregants to go out 'on their own' to make a significant impact in the lives of others." In addition, leaders of Extroverted Churches are more likely than leaders of other church types to select *contemporary* and *innovative* as the best words to describe their church.

4. Raving Fans of Their Church

People who attend Extroverted Churches really love their church. Satisfaction with four of the five Best Practice Principles is well above average, especially (not surprisingly) Pastor the Local Community (see Chart 4.2). Their overall satisfaction with how the church is "helping you grow" and with the senior pastor also is high. With so many raving fans, it is not surprising that two-thirds of Extroverted Churches report growth in weekend worship attendance over the past year.

5. Shallow on Scripture

One area where congregants in Extroverted Churches see room for improvement is with their church's efforts around Embedding the Bible. They would like to see their church do more to help them gain a deeper understanding of Scripture. Given the low levels of Bible reading and reflection at Extroverted Churches, it's mission-critical that this archetype's leaders balance their focus on serving with greater attention to helping congregants regularly interact with God's Word. Growth in core beliefs likely will follow as minds and hearts are transformed by the work of the Spirit.

6. East-Coast Urbanites

Compared to other church types, Extroverted Churches are much more likely to be located on the East Coast, especially in New England and the Southeast, and to be found in an urban setting. Extroverted

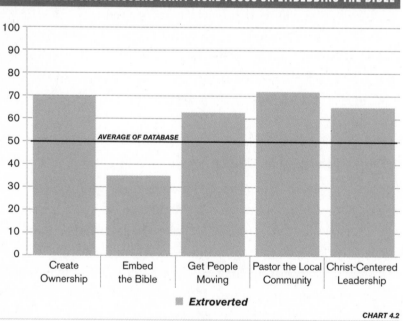

EXTROVERTED CHURCHGOERS WANT MORE FOCUS ON EMBEDDING THE BIBLE

AVERAGE OF DATABASE

Create Ownership | Embed the Bible | Get People Moving | Pastor the Local Community | Christ-Centered Leadership

■ *Extroverted*

CHART 4.2

Church congregants are also less likely to have an annual income of more than seventy-five thousand dollars or to have completed college. They tend, however, to be similar to other church types in their age distribution, racial/ethnic diversity, and average weekend worship attendance.

The following case study tells the story of Grace Community Church, which began its ministry as a church plant in the 1980s. By October 2008, when it became one of the first churches to take the REVEAL survey, it was quite well established in the Maryland/DC area. Grace fell into the Extroverted Church archetype—though not due to an exceptional service strategy like Epic's. Rather, its more modest (but average) profile of serving and evangelism looked impressive compared with its below-average beliefs and spiritual practices, particularly among those in its Exploring Christ segment. Grace congregants also expressed above-average satisfaction with the church and especially with their senior pastor, Mark Norman—two factors that are consistent with a typical Extroverted Church.

Aware of Grace's "Christianity Lite" reputation, Mark wasn't surprised when the survey confirmed that this reputation was likely deserved. This objective evidence prompted Mark and his leadership team to turn that state of affairs on its head.

AN EXTROVERTED-TO-ENERGIZED CASE STUDY: GRACE COMMUNITY CHURCH, FULTON, MARYLAND

For much of its twenty-eight-year history, Grace Community Church considered its attendance-makes-you-a-member attitude as a positive. It seemed welcoming. Uncomplicated. Inclusive. And practical, given the church's location between Baltimore and Washington, DC, amidst a highly educated, affluent, sophisticated citizenry that was neither

TROUBLED

COMPLACENT

EXTROVERTED

AVERAGE

INTROVERTED

SELF-MOTIVATED

ENERGIZED

VIBRANT

used to nor inclined to embrace an evangelical, nondenominational Protestant church plant.

Launched in Columbia, Maryland, in 1984, Grace joined a community that was predominantly Catholic in faith, as well as both politically and socially liberal. From the outset—as its congregation met in a progression of facilities from a basement to various schools to an office park and finally, in 2006, to its current church building—most new attenders were people who had moved to the East Coast from other parts of the nation.

"When our people come to us with an idea for church, if they brought that idea with them from Florida, Texas, or California, we tell them to go away," jokes Mark Norman. "That's how different our world is here." Then he gets serious: "We definitely are a subculture in our community because of our evangelical, Bible-based beliefs. So it can be tough."

Despite its challenges, Grace's growth was dramatic. As was the church's response to its first REVEAL survey, taken in October 2008.

Mark, who joined Grace as senior pastor in 1990 to lead the church's 140 attenders, says his elders are not only "very conscientious," but are, like their neighbors, highly qualified and gifted individuals "who are always asking, 'How are we doing?' They're like what author Jim Collins calls PNFs—paranoid neurotic freaks—constantly wondering, 'Are we really doing any good? Or are we just grabbing a crowd? What can we do better?'"

In efforts toward improvement, the church had self-surveyed its congregation in 2003. Then, five years later, when considering a second survey, they heard about REVEAL. "We decided we'd probably be better off using something that was already out there, thinking it would be easier for us to handle," Mark explains. "That's what got us in."

And how did they react, post-survey, to their initial Spiritual Vitality Index (SVI) score of 63? "It was really hard," Mark admits.

"For our PhDs and high achievers and professionals and all the rest of that, to be told we were in the sixtieth percentile or whatever—that just did not go over well. The optimists among us were pointing out all the things that were good, rejoicing over some things that could have been worse, while the glass-half-empty people were talking about how we had real work to do. This is a pretty take-the-world kind of crowd, so I don't think there was a lot of depression or any desire to quit and find something else to do. It was really more of a challenge, and our people were ready to take it on."

And take it on they did—starting with three leadership decisions.

Leadership Decision #1 was to shift from a philosophy of independence to unity.

"Through our first fifteen years, we'd been saying, 'Come worship with us and be part of our church, but do whatever God has called you to do,'" Mark explains. Now everyone was asked to join together in common purpose. "I think one of the big wake-up calls of our first REVEAL study was, 'We've got to move from everybody doing their own thing to doing some things together,'" Mark says. "That was a philosophical shift for us. And frankly, the old model was a little hard to take down."

Leadership Decision #2 was to create a new vision, based on the Great Commandment.

Focusing the soul of the church on "Love the Lord your God, and love your neighbor as yourself" started with addressing Grace's heretofore-unresolved definition of membership.

Leadership Decision #3 was to simplify discipleship.

Per Mark: "We had a list of things people should do to grow their relationship with Christ that even the staff couldn't remember. So we redefined *discipleship* around three relationships: your relationship with God, your relationship with people inside the church, and your relationship with those outside of the church. We drove everything through those three concepts. It's the most important thing we did."

Grace Got Their People Moving—Through Membership

With a new philosophy of doing things together, membership became more than mere attendance. Much more. "We talked about who we were and asked people to come be a part of that," Mark says. "We made it much more formal, telling people, 'Hey, if you want to belong here, give here, serve here, and get in a group here, you should become a Grace member.'"

The initial opportunity to do that took the form of a six-week Sunday morning message series—one that concluded with an invitation to approximately 1,600 attenders to declare, "I'm in." Subsequently, the content of that series became the basis for two three-hour membership workshops called First Steps.

When leaders first considered what membership-related topics to cover in First Steps, they assumed most content would relate directly to Grace. But they soon changed their minds, determining that it should focus primarily on God and the Word. Beneath the class's Love God and Love Others canopy, lessons focused on such things as small groups, Christian neighbors, and nonbelievers within the community and world. "We talk about money, about serving, about being part of the body," says Mark. "It includes a lot of content—and it really has some teeth to it."

Those who opt for membership agree to pursue eleven commitments—objectives ranging from being baptized to developing a personal devotional life to becoming part of a group. But Grace is far more focused on spiritual growth than on completing a checklist, and their small group system is the primary means to that end.

Grace Embedded the Bible and Created Ownership—
Through Small Groups

"Small groups became the primary place where pastoral care and discipleship were going to happen at Grace," says Mark. "Saying that up front has helped a lot. The importance of being in a group stepped up, in each and everyone's lives."

Certainly, small groups were available at Grace long before its REVEAL survey. But post-survey, Mark says Grace "increased the volume, in both intensity and frequency. In the past, you could get in a small group here, but it was really survival of the fittest. You had to call in and ask if we could find a place for you. Now, we launch groups three times a year and make a big deal about it. It's not uncommon to get a hundred to a hundred and twenty people in a room and start twenty new small groups on the spot."

It's not, however, just about the numbers.

Every fall, the entire church studies a common topic, something significant that the pastors and elders have determined will help move people forward in a particular spiritual area. For six to nine weeks, this topic is the basis not only for the weekend services, but for children's and youth classes—and all small groups. Then, for the rest of the year, groups are free to determine their own directions—although not randomly, but based on their own Spiritual Health Assessment.

This Spiritual Health Assessment measures members' progress against the three relationships that define discipleship for the church: relationship with Christ, relationship with others in the church, and impact on the world through relationships outside the church.

Then, depending on which area stands out as most in need of improvement, the group can choose from an impressive list of two- to three-month studies available through the church and endorsed by other groups with similar assessments.

Just as group members benefit from such specific direction, so do their leaders. While some of them are raised up from existing groups

TROUBLED COMPLACENT EXTROVERTED AVERAGE INTROVERTED SELF-MOTIVATED ENERGIZED VIBRANT and others are chosen for six-week leadership commitments by their newly formed groups, all are constantly supported by their coaches. In fact, Grace's coaches counsel with their group leaders at least once every ten days for the first twelve weeks of group life.

This ongoing reinforcement—through measurement, curriculum, and coaching support—of the three relationships that define discipleship for the church undoubtedly contributed to the increasing spiritual depth demonstrated by Grace's second REVEAL survey.

Two Years Later, Grace Assessed Their Progress

Two years into these and other initiatives, Grace was eager to learn how effectively they were addressing the issues raised by their initial REVEAL results. Not ones to sit still and wonder, the congregation took the survey again.

In short, the church's SVI climbed from 63 to 70—an impressive improvement, especially in so short a time. Closer inspection makes one even more inclined to send high fives their way, because improvements in several areas that church leaders specifically focused on are close to amazing.

Take small group participation, which increased from 55 to 64 percent overall and rose significantly in all four spiritual segments. Another very important, statistically meaningful shift occurred in the congregation's belief in a personal God, which is the most influential spiritual catalyst for those who are Growing in Christ. These new believers, at 39 percent, represent the largest spiritual segment at Grace. Also noteworthy was the statistically meaningful increase in the more mature Close to Christ group—to 29 percent of the congregation. And personal spiritual practices increased across the board.

What significantly decreased? Well, the number of congregants who described themselves as "Stalled," for one thing, dropping from 17 percent to 10 percent. Grace Community Church clearly considers itself a church on the move.

To where? That has yet to be seen. But encouraged by the Grace congregation's willing support of its leaders' direction, Mark and his team are busy with initiatives to accelerate spiritual momentum. Since 2010, they have formed a "deeper team" to propose ideas for taking congregants deeper spiritually. They've scheduled a number of events—like a Walk Thru the Bible series, a seminar on atheism, and a workshop on Bible translations. During our most recent conversation with Grace leaders, the church was in the midst of a thirty-four-week journey through Romans.

When asked what a long-term congregant would say is different at Grace now compared to two years ago, Mark turns reflective. "The rap on us used to be that we were Christianity Lite," he says. "No one would say that about us today."

THE HOPE FOR THE EXTROVERTED CHURCH

Excited, eager to please, ready to chase down whatever gets thrown their way—the faith of Extroverted Church congregants is like the trust and high spirits of rambunctious puppies. They're somewhat awkward, not quite sure about boundaries or obligations, but they are revved up to go wherever they are led. The challenge is to point them in the right direction.

The right direction—and a touch of discipline—is also the remedy for the Extroverted Church. Newcomers—those far from God, and those fallen away and disappointed by traditional church—are pouring through their doors, inspired by the church's reputation for delivering something different and challenging. The opportunity is to meet or exceed that expectation by providing them with a taste of spiritual life that both galvanizes them into service *and* puts them on a path to fall in love with Jesus.

Mark Norman's Grace Community Church created the "right direction" by focusing its energy on membership and creating First Steps. At

TROUBLED

COMPLACENT

EXTROVERTED

AVERAGE

INTROVERTED

SELF-MOTIVATED

ENERGIZED

VIBRANT

Symptoms of an Extroverted Church

A church likely falls into the Extroverted Church archetype if these three primary characteristics exist:

1. *Congregants are spiritually immature.* Pastors would not be surprised to learn that many congregants don't agree with some of the core Christian beliefs, like salvation by grace or the Trinity—or that congregants struggle to define those core beliefs with any degree of accuracy. It's also doubtful that many Extroverted Church congregants pray and/or practice Bible study outside of an organized church setting.
2. *Energy and enthusiasm for community service abound in the church culture.* Congregants give unselfishly of their time and energy to whatever community-service challenge the church offers. Church leaders spend substantial time and resources considering which local (and global) issues to tackle with community-service initiatives.
3. *Congregants are happy with the church and its leadership.* Church leaders perceive a high level of satisfaction, sensing that people appreciate the spiritual guidance provided by the church and are confident the church is being well led.

Epic, IV Marsh encourages newcomers to proceed immediately into Equip, a two-and-a-half-hour newcomer class that introduces them to the church's point of view about how to experience faith through worship, in daily life, in teams, and in service to the community.

But there's no need to start from scratch. Beacon Church in Long Island, another high-energy Extroverted Church, introduced Alpha to its growing membership of three hundred young professionals, many of whom work in Manhattan. Despite commuting demands, more than one hundred people showed up every Tuesday night to wrestle with questions of faith through the ten-week Alpha curriculum.

The objective of these programs is to make it crystal clear to those who are new, as well as veterans who may need to be reminded, that the goal of the church is to help them grow into a disciple of Christ—*not* to plug them into a myriad of serving opportunities, as laudable as that may be.

A noteworthy postscript is that these orientation programs can subsequently flow into small group systems. At Grace, small group participation increased from 54 to 65 percent during the time between its two surveys (as compared to a REVEAL norm of 50 percent). At Beacon, small group participation is 62 percent; at Epic, it's 71 percent. This migration into community life is reminiscent of the "granddaddy" of church orientation strategies—the Purpose Driven baseball diamond, known for giving newcomers a taste of church vision, serving opportunities, spiritual disciplines, and then small group connections.[2] It is not uncommon to find a modified version of the Purpose Driven model operating in the most spiritually vital churches in the REVEAL database.

This is the hope of the Extroverted Church: to jump-start the spiritual lives of their new-to-faith people in a powerful way by establishing expectations about what the life of a Christ follower looks like—and by making it clear that helping them achieve that life is the highest priority of the church.

GRACE COMMUNITY CHURCH: 2014 UPDATE

What's the single biggest difference in Grace Community Church since the case study?
Grace Community has become a more unified spiritual body, due to a pair of unfortunate circumstances beginning with the tragic, unexpected death of the church's worship leader in November 2013. This long-standing and highly visible leader left behind a heartbroken family and congregation.

---

[2] Rick Warren, *The Purpose Driven Church* (Grand Rapids: Zondervan, 1995), 144.

TROUBLED

COMPLACENT

EXTROVERTED

AVERAGE

INTROVERTED

SELF-MOTIVATED

ENERGIZED

VIBRANT

A few months later, two senior ministry leaders were let go due to moral failure. When asked how Grace responded to these back-to-back traumas, senior pastor Mark Norman says, "We leaned into them." Key ministry activities were canceled as the church body publicly "embraced the grieving" together, and Mark believes the congregation's relational and spiritual bonds grew stronger as a result.

What's new in the church's discipleship strategies and culture since the case study?

One essential step taken in the wake of Grace Community's dual crises was to introduce a biweekly "point leader" meeting that operates absent an agenda, providing a forum to air ministry concerns and discuss current issues. Initially launched after the death of their worship leader, Mark says the meetings create a leadership cohesion that's been particularly important in their current circumstances.

Grace has also strengthened its small groups by identifying and building into leaders in advance of each church campaign, and Mark reports its First Steps membership class continues to be "very well received," although it's now less information-oriented and more focused on introducing key leaders and their priorities. The goal, according to Mark, is to inspire people to "sign up for a movement."

Grace took its third REVEAL survey in October 2013, which confirmed this Energized Church's spiritual strength—strength that undoubtedly helped them weather the storms that came their way.

What's next on the horizon for Grace Community Church?

Like so many churches led by baby-boomer pastors, Grace Community's primary concern is succession planning—particularly given the recent loss of three ministry leaders. Mark says he's hoping to identify internal replacements for a number of positions, including his senior pastor role, so that a transition can take place over the next three to five years.

TROUBLED

COMPLACENT

EXTROVERTED

AVERAGE

INTROVERTED

SELF-MOTIVATED

ENERGIZED

VIBRANT

CHAPTER 5

THE AVERAGE CHURCH

"Will it play in Peoria?"

Coined in the days of vaudeville, this famous catchphrase pegs Peoria, Illinois, as a microcosm of America—the archetype for "Average Town, USA." From its midsize population, to its location virtually in the center of the country, to its dependence on the farming industry, Peoria was considered one of the most ordinary, unremarkable communities in the nation.

Compared to its legendary "average" past, however, present-day Peoria reflects a less clear-cut reality. Nowadays consumer-brand test marketers and political pollsters are more likely to show up in Boise, Idaho, or Albany, New York, to "take the pulse" of America. Peoria's Main Street image is taking a beating as street crime, unemployment, and poverty rates rise above the US average, and its demographic mix becomes less reflective of America's mainstream.

Average Churches share Peoria's bland facade of commonplace

statistics, and they also face more complicated issues that lie beneath the surface. A small church in Ontario, Canada, provides an example. Its under-one-hundred weekend attenders delivered a solid 71 Spiritual Vitality Index in its REVEAL report, a score right at the peak of the bell-shaped curve featured in all statistics textbooks. *Everything* was average—including congregants' spiritual beliefs, attitudes, and behaviors—as well as how they felt about the job their church was doing to help them grow their relationship with Christ.

But one issue did break through this statistical monotone. When asked about several unfavorable statistics related to the church's worship experience, the senior pastor responds with a laugh. "Worship wars!" he explains, referencing the rivalry among local churches when it comes to musical prowess. Due to the limited talent pool in its small congregation, "We're down to two pianos, and that's about it," he says. But the issue, in his mind, goes deeper. "We live in an image-driven town," the pastor explains. "I call it 'Fluffyville.'" He feels his greatest challenge is to set aside the image issues in order to engage people more deeply in their relationship with Christ through personal spiritual practices. He is trying to drive this home with a ten-ten-ten strategy: ten minutes in prayer and ten minutes in Scripture every day, plus ten conversations with different people about Jesus every week. He says he sees signs of progress.

Another Average Church, this one with Quaker roots near Cleveland, fielded its second REVEAL survey—and scored its *second* Spiritual Vitality Index of 69. This SVI—like the Canadian church's 71—put them at the dead center of "average," and except for a couple of specific areas, their report was curiously unchanged from their results two years earlier.

But beneath the surface were signs of a damaged church culture, possibly in the early stages of recovery. For example, the report showed that out of a laundry list of options, congregants chose "maintain harmony" as one of the top priorities for the senior pastor—which is typically a sign of church unrest. Sure enough, eight years earlier the church had parted with its longtime senior pastor in a traumatic split, and then drifted for five years before finding its current leader. "They're still getting used to me," he says.

It's clear that this new pastor has not been idle. Small group participation and satisfaction rocketed up between the two reports as he transitioned the church from a traditional Sunday school model to a small group system. The pastor is also clearly pleased that the percentage of people participating in a weekly faith-based activity *outside* of the normal Sunday experience has more than tripled, to 60 percent, compared with two years ago. "Our people love to be together," he says, sounding amused but maybe a bit exasperated—because clinging to large-group experiences could deter progress as he tries to embed a new discipleship strategy: Gather, Grow, and Go! (Suggesting, perhaps, that Gather has been achieved, so it is time to Grow. And Go.)

These churches and many more like them prove an undeniable truth about the Average Church—that "average" isn't the whole story. This is encouraging news because the Average Church diagnosis is one of the least popular archetypes to communicate to a senior pastor, for two reasons. The first is reflected in the well-known anonymous quote: "Everyone wants to be normal, but no one wants to be average." Most of the time, Average Church pastors are dismayed by the idea that their church's spiritual vitality is no better than run-of-the-mill, thinking that perhaps this means the church's spiritual offerings are mediocre, even boring.

The second reason this archetype is so unpopular is that it's almost always a surprise. That's understandable, because on the surface Average Churches have a lot going for them. Often almost half of their congregants are happy new believers who sign up for whatever church activities are offered. So the Average Church culture seems to bustle with spiritual enthusiasm and energy—possibly lulling pastors

TROUBLED

COMPLACENT

EXTROVERTED

AVERAGE

INTROVERTED

SELF-MOTIVATED

ENERGIZED

VIBRANT

into thinking congregants are cruising along at a steady pace toward spiritual maturity.

Therein lies the danger for the Average Church. All those happy voices engaged in multiple activities can mask the reality that their spiritual lives are more stagnant than vital—defined more by a growing engagement *with their church* than a growing relationship with Jesus. While this circumstance occurs in other archetypes, Average Church pastors seem uniquely blindsided by this conclusion—which suggests the solution for "average" lies not in the launch of a big Bible-based campaign, nor in a full-throttle push into community service. The solution rests with leaders who are willing to take the blinders off and seek the source of "average"— which lies within them.

ALL CHURCHES CAST "SHADOWS"

Each church archetype is built on a rock-solid foundation of statistics, with its characteristics rigorously nailed down by data from thousands of congregants and hundreds of stories collected from REVEAL client churches. However, when the light of this research shines on an individual church, sometimes its archetype "fit" is inexact. In other words, churches often cast "shadows"—displaying the characteristics of *two* archetypes, the first as the primary fit and a second that is the next best descriptor for the church's characteristics. Identifying and understanding this shadow archetype can enrich the insights for church leaders about next steps that might be most effective for their congregants, and that's especially helpful for Average Churches.

Average Church "Shadows" Add Strategic Depth and Diversity
Being told your church is "average" is not particularly helpful, because that description does not identify strengths or weaknesses. Conse-

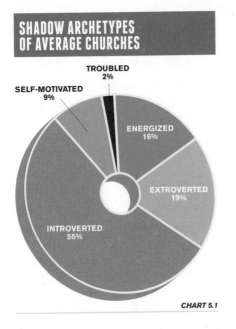

SHADOW ARCHETYPES OF AVERAGE CHURCHES

TROUBLED 2%

SELF-MOTIVATED 9%

ENERGIZED 16%

EXTROVERTED 19%

INTROVERTED 55%

CHART 5.1

quently, there is no clear-cut pathway for improvement—no strengths to build on or weaknesses to minimize. So it's not surprising that Average Churches struggle to determine which strategic path will most likely break them out of spiritual ordinariness. Shadow archetypes, therefore, were developed primarily to help Average Churches. As Chart 5.1 shows, their most common secondary archetype is the Introverted Church, the second best fit for 55 percent of Average Churches. The Extroverted Church and Energized Church archetypes account for the lion's share of secondary patterns of the remaining Average Churches. Only 9 percent of Average Churches have a Self-Motivated shadow, and just a few have the Troubled archetype as their shadow archetype.

Understanding their shadow archetype gives Average Churches more insight into options that might accelerate spiritual growth in their congregations. For example, the Cleveland-area church described earlier in this chapter has the Introverted Church as its shadow. This makes sense based on the pastor's description of his congregation's historic preference for doing Bible studies in large-group Sunday school settings. Knowing this "introverted" side of his congregation's spiritual personality gives the pastor another avenue to pursue for strategies since it's likely that an initiative effective in Introverted Churches—for example, a spiritual mentoring process—would also work in his Average Church circumstances.

TROUBLED

COMPLACENT

EXTROVERTED

AVERAGE

INTROVERTED

SELF-MOTIVATED

ENERGIZED

VIBRANT

"Shadows" Foretell Church Futures

Each one of the eight archetypes has one or two shadows, which are listed in Table 5.1. Those shadows generally share some of the characteristics of the primary archetype. For example, Complacent Churches are similar to both Troubled Churches and Extroverted Churches in their lower measures of spiritual growth markers (such as lower personal spiritual practices), so it makes sense that these two archetypes are the most common shadows for Complacent Churches.

PRIMARY ARCHETYPE	SHADOW ARCHETYPES
Troubled	Complacent (45%); Introverted (34%)
Complacent	Troubled (51%); Extroverted (28%)
Introverted	Average (67%)
Average	Introverted (55%)
Extroverted	Energized (44%); Average (34%)
Energized	Extroverted (51%); Vibrant (22%)
Self-Motivated	Vibrant (41%); Introverted (36%)
Vibrant	Self-Motivated (52%); Energized (42%)

TABLE 5.1

Shadow archetypes represent the most likely future trajectories for churches. For example, an Extroverted Church that takes steps to help congregants engage more intentionally in spiritual growth is likely to move into the Energized archetype (its most common shadow). By the same token, Extroverted Churches that are less intentional in their efforts may drift toward the Average archetype. In a similar way, Self-Motivated Churches can move forward into the Vibrant Church archetype or allow themselves to slide into an Introverted Church pattern. Knowing their shadow archetypes can help churches determine which next steps are most likely to ignite spiritual energy and momentum.

Legacy Church offers a case study on how shadow archetypes can foretell a church's future. In its first REVEAL survey, Legacy fit the

Average Church archetype to a T. Nothing was going particularly badly at the church, but neither did anything stand out as going remarkably well. However, the impressive—even brave—steps the church took in response to their REVEAL results fast-tracked their movement into the Energized archetype, which—not surprisingly—had been their shadow archetype in the original survey.

AN AVERAGE-TO-ENERGIZED CASE STUDY: LEGACY CHURCH, PLANO, TEXAS

Imagine the nation's seventieth most populous city—one named, in 2006, as the best place to live in the United States. Note that 53 percent of this city's residents have at least a bachelor's degree and that in 2007 *CNN Money* ranked it the wealthiest city in the US, with a median average income of over seventy-seven thousand dollars. Then consider that in 2010, *Forbes* magazine named it the safest American city of 250,000 or more, that its schools consistently rank among the best in the nation, and that its unemployment rate is half the national average.

So where's the challenge? Well, in all of the above. Because while Plano, Texas, appears to have "a church on every corner," only about 30 percent of its self-reliant, self-assured residents attend services. "It's a pretty remarkable place," says Legacy Church's senior pastor, Gene Wilkes. "But even though we're in the Bible Belt, where there is a strong subculture of churched Christians, the majority of people are not. And as the rest of the culture has shifted away from its need and dependence upon faith and the church, that's been particularly true here in Plano." Despite its dynamic, dedicated staff, plenty of resources, and twenty-five years as part of the city, Legacy Church's leaders suspected it should be doing more to foster its people's spiritual growth.

TROUBLED

COMPLACENT

EXTROVERTED

AVERAGE

INTROVERTED

SELF-MOTIVATED

ENERGIZED

VIBRANT

In the past, Legacy had used Natural Church Development resources to determine how they fared in this area; then, while attending the 2008 Willow Creek Leadership Summit, they heard about REVEAL. "We hadn't assessed our spiritual growth for years, so we needed a kind of baseline of where we were," Gene says. "When Willow put REVEAL together, it was something we knew we could use." So in March 2010, Legacy took its first survey.

Clearly, the more than three hundred adults in the congregation were on board, with an almost unheard-of response rate of 62 percent. What they had to say, though, was somewhat less impressive. While satisfaction with the senior pastor was strong at 78 percent, only 58 percent were satisfied with weekend services and even fewer (49 percent) were satisfied with the church's role in their spiritual growth. Only 15 percent read their Bible daily, and 13 percent acknowledged they were spiritually "stalled." In short, Legacy Church, despite (or maybe, in part, due to?) its extraordinary community, generated survey results that could best be defined as . . . *ordinary*.

"To be honest, I think REVEAL told many of us what we already knew," says life group pastor Tammy Dillon. "But we needed tangible figures to substantiate that. So when REVEAL confirmed that we had a fairly biblically illiterate congregation, it just affirmed that we needed to do some definite work in that area."

To launch that work, Legacy created a Spiritual Growth Team, made up of the pastoral team and a leadership team including congregants and staff. At first, the groups met separately, discussing what they'd learned about spiritual growth, the insights Legacy's survey had uncovered, and what the church's priorities should become. Then the two teams joined forces—and made two key leadership decisions.

Leadership Decision #1 was to boldly and clearly define discipleship.

They used REVEAL's spiritual growth continuum, calling it "The Way," and renaming its four levels of spiritual maturity to more closely align with Legacy's culture and language. Retaining the initial segment descriptions of Exploring Christ and Growing in Christ, the third and fourth segments became Living with Christ and Dying for Christ.

Gene admits that the team wrestled for quite a while with the *Dying for Christ* description, but concluded that it best represented the ultimate perspective—the "if you will come after me, deny yourself, take up your cross, and follow me" perspective—of this most spiritually mature segment. The team felt this bold description could be especially meaningful to the members of their prosperous, goal-oriented community. The idea that following Christ requires a willingness to sacrifice everything for him is difficult to accept in a community that is barely scraping by. It can be even more challenging when the community's success results in a lifestyle of abundance.

Leadership Decision #2 was to produce a menu of options for moving along "The Way."

Legacy's segment descriptions set the stage for spiritual growth, but its leaders knew that stepping up the urgency and challenge of discipleship wasn't enough. They also had to ramp up the number and quality of growth opportunities so Legacy's people could see a path that would, in fact, help them make progress along "The Way."

Not surprisingly, that path of opportunities started with the Bible.

Legacy Embedded the Bible—with a "Buzz" of Creative Ways to Engage in Scripture

In response to the low number of its congregants who had reported spending time in the Bible, Legacy was determined to make this a fundamental practice throughout the church—for everyone from preschoolers to adults and across activities ranging from life groups to Sunday sermons. Common to all of these audiences and initiatives would be Zondervan's newly released book *The Story*. "In the

TROUBLED

COMPLACENT

EXTROVERTED

AVERAGE

INTROVERTED

SELF-MOTIVATED

ENERGIZED

VIBRANT

fall of 2010, when we got our REVEAL results back, we also found this book," Tammy says. "It came to our door a month before we were about to gear up life groups again. God literally landed it in our lap—like *boom*, in our lap! So we threw out what we were going to do and said, 'No, *this* is God's answer to how we are going to help our people understand the Bible.'"

Here, too, the staff adapted this resource to Legacy's congregation. ("That's kind of what we do," Gene says, laughing.) They divided the book's contents into segments to cover all twelve months of 2011, and then broke the material down into six daily reading assignments per week. And for those who didn't want to carry a book around all year? "They could get a daily e-mail to read—all they had to do was click on it," says Tammy. "Or they could even listen to the material on their smartphones—it would speak the assignment out loud to them on their way to work or while they were carpooling their children."

And the children? They were equally engaged, as children's director Markus Lloyd's team purposefully and creatively kept them in the Word right alongside their parents. "For the kids to really understand this, we thought they would need to be learning the same things as their parents," he says. "So we looked for the best way to input the Bible into the home that would keep every age group talking about the same things—whether that was at dinnertime, in the car leaving church, or whenever they were together."

The result was a Family Notebook covering the entire year. For every week, it provided the Scripture being discussed in Sunday's service as well as a story synopsis, the story's main point, and the best ways to enter a discussion of the story. It also included questions appropriate for different age groups—preschoolers, elementary, and youth—to launch family-wide discussions. "We made that available to every family for the first semester—January until June," Markus says. "During the summer we gave them some other things to do, then we went back with some new pages for their notebooks in the fall."

But the spiritual "buzz" at Legacy extended well beyond *The Story.* They also launched Legacy U, a classroom-like teaching time offered before Sunday services. Not surprisingly, the first class it offered—named The Biggest Loser—focused on the Dying-for-Christ level of spiritual maturity.

In addition to Legacy U, in early 2012 the church also began to provide extended prayer time *following* Sunday services. This increased emphasis on personal prayer coincided with Sunday sermons and life-group studies based on this key spiritual practice. "We didn't have a 'How to Pray' class or anything like that," Gene says. "Instead our spring emphasis was Jesus' prayer life in the book of Luke. We let Christ in the Gospels be the example that guided our church-wide emphasis."

Life groups have long been highly valued and extremely well attended at Legacy Church, with participation at 89 percent, compared to a much lower 50 percent average among all surveyed churches. These less formal gatherings, which are based on participant interaction more than leader-led teaching, provided an ideal opportunity to explore the topic of prayer. For example, in February 2012, in addition to the newly available Sunday morning prayer time, Legacy's life groups launched a twelve-week series on the Lord's Prayer. Once again they provided e-mails and other encouragements. And once again they fostered family discussions by overflowing the topic into children's ministry in some very tangible, experiential ways.

Legacy Pastored the Local Community—by Freeing Up Time and Finding Partners

Unlike Bible engagement, which offered huge potential for growth, Legacy's REVEAL-prompted serving initiative was more a combination of renewed focus and refinement. "A value we've held for a long time is 'You're most like Jesus when you serve,'" Gene explains. Now, though, congregants would broaden that value by serving "in the church, through the church, and on my own." Specifically, they would move more of their serving off campus and into their community. While the children's ministry continues to depend on its volunteers, various other in-church programs were curtailed, freeing up time for more "through the church" options. "We started looking toward partnering with other churches to take some things out in the street where the people are," Markus explains.

It hasn't been easy, but Legacy's success in this effort speaks for itself. Instead of holding its annual Fall Festival, something many Plano churches do each year, Legacy suggested joining forces in 2011. Although it took a tremendous amount of coordination and collaboration, several churches agreed, holding a joint festival at a local school and contributing the event proceeds to an area food pantry. Building on this success, Markus recruited half a dozen area churches to serve in "Love Where You Live," a weekend cleanup effort in partnership with city government, during which church volunteers picked up trash, repaired homes, and otherwise served an area of Plano that Markus describes as "needing some love."

Then Pine Cove, a big Christian camp in Texas that takes its camp to a church campus each summer, asked Legacy if they would be the host church in the summer of 2012. "We were like, 'Well, our kids in this area just go to camps all summer long,'" says Markus. "'What if we partnered with a couple other churches and took the camp to the lower-income area of our city—and then scholarshiped all the kids who wanted to attend?'" Four Plano churches did exactly that, sending their volunteers to serve about seventy kids who otherwise would never have had such an opportunity.

Two Years Later, Legacy Checked on Its Progress

In the midst of its response to its initial REVEAL survey, Legacy opted to check its progress with a follow-up survey in March 2012. The result was encouraging trajectories across the board. Satisfaction with the church's role in spiritual growth rose dramatically from 49 to 65 percent, for instance. And dissatisfaction plummeted from 21 to 12 percent. The stalled percentage dropped from 13 percent to 8. And what about that all-important area of spiritual growth? The Growing in Christ segment, formerly at 47 percent, dropped to 41—because Legacy's Living with Christ and Dying for Christ segments grew in statistically meaningful ways, from 23 to 27 and from 24 to 29 percent, respectively.

Such movement not only affirms the church's bold new descriptions of spiritual maturity but also generates respect for members of Legacy's congregation—who, even in light of their secular success, are now stepping up to embrace a "to die is gain" definition of *eternal* success.

THE HOPE FOR THE AVERAGE CHURCH

While visiting Chicago, a pastor from South Africa asked to meet with the REVEAL team in person to talk through his survey results. Initially the report showed no obvious cause for concern. But then the conversation took an emotional and difficult turn because, while nothing was clearly wrong, the spiritual heart of this Average Church was weak. Pages of statistics measuring spiritual attitudes, beliefs, and behaviors showed no variation from the norm. Like many other Average Churches, the report for this church reflected a statistical "flatline"—which means it was in a state of little to no spiritual progress or advancement.

The South African pastor seemed discouraged but unsurprised by these observations. Tears welled up in his eyes as he recounted a recent retreat where he and his staff prayerfully tried to discern God's

TROUBLED

COMPLACENT

EXTROVERTED

AVERAGE

INTROVERTED

SELF-MOTIVATED

ENERGIZED

VIBRANT

Symptoms of an Average Church

A church likely falls into the Average Church archetype if these three primary characteristics exist:

1. *Congregants' spiritual lives are more church-centered than Christ-centered.* Pastors suspect that underneath the busyness of church activities there is little follow-through into the everyday lives of congregants. In other words, pastors would agree with the observation that their people define their spiritual journey almost exclusively in terms of church engagement.
2. *Pastors sense more spiritual contentedness than passion among church leaders.* Staff meetings are routinely dominated by operational discussions. Church leaders rarely gather—officially or unofficially—for authentic spiritual community. Senior church leaders would acknowledge that their relationships lack spiritual passion and accountability.
3. *Little sets the church apart from other churches in the community.* Pastors would be hard pressed to name a handful of real church distinctions, particularly in the context of spiritual formation. The phrase "so-so" would ring all too true: so-so worship experience, so-so spiritual community, so-so biblical literacy, and so forth.

direction for his church. "We all reached the same conclusion," he said sadly. "Like the church in Ephesus (Revelation 2:4), we had lost our way. We had lost our first love."

The hope for the Average Church is that its leaders will reach that same conclusion—because the fault for its lackluster spirituality lies squarely with them. They've become accustomed to happy congregational feedback that masks the truth that the faith walk of their people is stuck in the mire of church activities. Based on countless consultations, the toxin plaguing Average Churches—and its antidote—is leadership.

When Average Church leaders face that truth, they will hopefully set aside preaching agendas, operational demands, and the everyday pressures of doing ministry to revisit—*and revive*—the collective passion that drew them into serving Jesus and his church in the first place. Because when that desire is reignited, Average Churches everywhere can move to new and much more powerful levels of impact.

"I know your deeds, your hard work and your perseverance" (Revelation 2:2). These encouraging words from Christ to the church of Ephesus should reassure Average Churches because they, too, lead active, productive ministries. Then they should heed these words of warning that follow, recalled by the South African pastor: "Yet I hold this against you: You have forsaken the love you had at first" (v. 4).

This caution applies not only to Average Churches but also to leaders in all the archetypes. It's a reminder not to allow the busyness and burdens of ministry to overpower the love for Jesus that inspired them to devote their lives to his church. Because when that happens, they risk spiritual stagnation. They risk leading a church that's busy but spiritually flat.

Worst of all, in the service of Christ, they risk being "Average."

LEGACY CHURCH: 2014 UPDATE

What's the single biggest difference in Legacy Church since the case study?

Legacy has experienced two major transitions. First, after serving as Legacy's senior pastor for twenty-five years, Gene Wilkes left in 2013 to become president of the B. H. Carroll Theological Seminary. Today's senior pastor, thirty-two-year-old Kevin Boyd, brings thirteen years of ministry experience—including two church plants—and a passion for young families and strong church relationship networks.

The second transition reflects Legacy's increasingly multicultural community, prompted by large numbers of Asian employees arriving to work in various corporate headquarters—including Toyota, which

TROUBLED

COMPLACENT

EXTROVERTED

AVERAGE

INTROVERTED

SELF-MOTIVATED

ENERGIZED

VIBRANT

recently announced the relocation of its US headquarters to Plano. This shift has transformed the predominantly WASP community to a multi-lingual, multiethnic society with a growing non-Christian influence.

What's new in Legacy's discipleship strategies and culture since the case study?

"You're a missionary with a corporate sponsor," says life groups pastor Tammy Dillon, offering a sound-bite description of Legacy's vision to equip its largely corporate-employed congregants to live out Christ's purpose for their lives. The message of "mission" accelerated with a one-year teaching plunge into the book of Acts following the church's second REVEAL survey, which Kevin recently complemented with a twenty-week dive into the book of Matthew. Influenced by the growing number of non-Christians in Plano, he says, "Our mission is all about the gospel. Because people here may not be needy, but they don't know Jesus."

What's next on the horizon for Legacy Church?

True to the church and its pastor's passion for connections, life groups are positioned as the conduit for everything. Kevin says a number equal to Legacy's adult worshiping attendance of three hundred now participate in life groups. The church's goal is to integrate children into life groups, with an initiative focused on spiritual gifts. The underlying intent is to begin a church-wide conversation about trusting Christ—rather than a career, profession, sport, or college—to define one's identity. This is a strategy that's very consistent with equipping "missionaries with a corporate sponsor."

CHAPTER 6

THE INTROVERTED CHURCH

What does our sixteenth president, Abraham Lincoln, have in common with Michael Jordan, arguably the greatest basketball player of all time? And what could the two of them possibly have in common with David Letterman? J. K. Rowling? Warren Buffett? Christina Aguilera?

On the surface, these famous people couldn't be more different in terms of their talents and life callings. But by reputation, they share one important characteristic: Along with an estimated one-third to one-half of the American population, they were/are introverts.[1]

None of these individuals fit the introvert stereotype of a shy, retiring wallflower. All are recognized leaders in their fields, known for challenging the status quo and admired for their focus and determination—traits reflecting a strength of character that is not atypical for an introverted personality, and is critical to understanding the Introverted Church.

For an Introverted Church, this strength of character is found in its

---

[1] Susan Cain, *Quiet: The Power of Introverts in a World That Can't Stop Talking* (New York: Broadway Paperbacks, 2012), 3.

77

TROUBLED
COMPLACENT
EXTROVERTED
AVERAGE
INTROVERTED
SELF-MOTIVATED
ENERGIZED
VIBRANT

deeply rooted faith. Congregants embrace the core Christian beliefs, such as belief in the personal presence of God and in the authority of the Bible to influence and guide their lives. They understand they are on a journey to develop a relationship with Christ, and they invest time and energy in spiritual practices to grow that relationship. They search Scripture regularly, likely because they are encouraged to do so by a church where the Bible is central to its teaching and culture.

This established pattern of Christian habits and values makes the diagnosis of an Introverted Church a tough pill to swallow for its leaders. After all, their people show many signs of spiritual maturity and seem to be authentically incorporating their walk with Jesus into their daily lives. Mark Ashton, senior pastor of the flagship Christian and Missionary Alliance church in Omaha (an Introverted Church with an initial SVI of 63), described it this way: "Getting that feedback was one of the most depressing moments of my ministry career." In fact, he kept his REVEAL results under wraps for three weeks, concerned how his church elders might respond.

This disappointment is understandable, but the reality is that pastors of Introverted Churches should be more encouraged than upset. That's because an Introverted Church has greater potential than any other archetype to make dramatic advances in spiritual vitality (which is exactly what happened in the case of the Omaha church). This makes sense, since the most important cornerstones for spiritual growth are already in place. As noted earlier, Introverted Church congregants buy into the core beliefs and also understand that they should spend time in prayer and Scripture on a regular basis. They are aware that a spiritual journey exists and that they are accountable to some extent for the speed of its movement.

So what's missing? That factor is found in the definition of an introvert: "a person characterized by concern primarily with his or her own thoughts and feelings," rather than with the external environment.[2]

---

[2] *Random House Dictionary*, s.v. "introvert."

Another spin on the introverted personality is to understand its source of energy. Introverts tend to recharge their batteries by being alone so they can contemplate the meaning of events and circumstances. In contrast, an extroverted personality recharges through activities and socializing with others. But—when considering what this implies about next steps for the Introverted Church—we must be careful not to leap to the conclusion that creating an expansive menu of serving opportunities or cracking the evangelism whip is the "prescription" for greater spiritual vitality. That's part of the answer, but it's not the cure.

For some insight, let's turn back to Michael Jordan, who was unable—though he tried—to migrate his athletic prowess from extraordinary achievements in professional basketball championships to success in major league baseball. The takeaway from this imperfect metaphor is that changing behaviors—trying harder—is unlikely to change the natural wiring of a human being. A person with a great jump shot may not have the skills to become a home-run hitter. In other words, layering on new behavior requirements is not a recipe for transformation.

Transformation, in fact, is what's missing at the Introverted Church, and the source of that transformation is the Holy Spirit. It's not about changing behaviors or trying harder. It's about a spiritual awakening—or as Dallas Willard put it so well, a renovation of the heart. It's about challenging people to reconsider and uproot long-established thoughts and feelings about the life Christ requires of his followers— "Whoever wants to be my disciple must deny themselves and take up their cross and follow me" (Matthew 16:24)—and then to live up to those demands.

The good news for Introverted Churches everywhere is that the Omaha church—along with the church featured in this chapter's case study and many others that have "stepped up to the plate" (to extend the sports analogy)—has proven that this kind of heart change is possible.

SEVEN FACTORS THAT SET THE INTROVERTED CHURCH APART

1. Established Believers

Congregants in Introverted Churches have very strong convictions about core Christian beliefs like salvation by grace and the authority of Scripture. On average, 55 percent are in the Close to Christ and Christ-Centered stages of spiritual growth (see Chart 1.2). Nearly 40 percent have attended their church for ten years or longer.

2. More Mary than Martha

As a whole, the congregation of an Introverted Church is diligent about making time for reflection on Scripture, prayer, and other spiritual practices. But there's a disconnect between what they are absorbing in their time with the Lord and their ability and/or willingness to act on it. Their faith-in-action behaviors (like evangelism and serving those in need) fall far short of what we would expect to see, given their levels of beliefs and spiritual practices. On average,

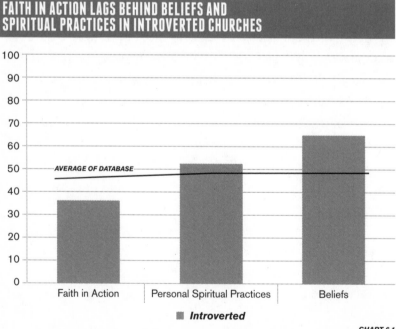

FAITH IN ACTION LAGS BEHIND BELIEFS AND SPIRITUAL PRACTICES IN INTROVERTED CHURCHES

AVERAGE OF DATABASE

Faith in Action · Personal Spiritual Practices · Beliefs

■ *Introverted*

CHART 6.1

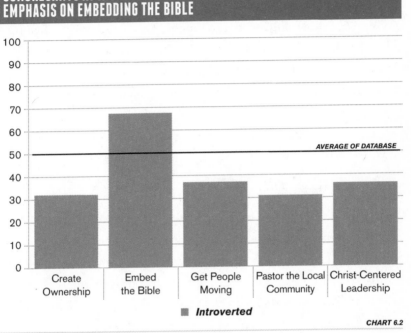

CONGREGANTS AT INTROVERTED CHURCHES APPRECIATE EMPHASIS ON EMBEDDING THE BIBLE

AVERAGE OF DATABASE

Create Ownership · Embed the Bible · Get People Moving · Pastor the Local Community · Christ-Centered Leadership

■ *Introverted*

CHART 6.2

TROUBLED

COMPLACENT

EXTROVERTED

AVERAGE

INTROVERTED

SELF-MOTIVATED

ENERGIZED

VIBRANT

just one in five Introverted Church congregants are having spiritual conversations with unchurched friends on a regular basis, and only 12 percent say they feel equipped to share their faith. Chart 6.1 compares Introverted Churches to the average on all three aspects of spiritual growth, showing how faith-in-action behaviors lag behind beliefs and spiritual practices.

3. Serious About Scripture

When you walk into an Introverted Church, expect to see lots of people carrying well-worn Bibles. The Embed the Bible principle is one that the Introverted Church has wholeheartedly embraced and implemented. In fact, they likely could offer suggestions to churches that struggle in this area. Chart 6.2 shows that Introverted Church congregations are highly satisfied with how their church integrates Scripture into everything they do.

4. Showing Signs of Unrest

The news on satisfaction with the church goes downhill at this point, as Chart 6.2 shows. Introverted Churches are second only to Troubled Churches in their dissatisfaction with their senior pastor, with their church's role in their spiritual growth, and with four of the Best Practice Principles. Given that congregants in Introverted Churches typically are in the more mature stages of spiritual growth, their dissatisfaction may be a sign of a need to step away from depending on the church to give them everything they need to grow.

5. Growing Stagnant

Instead of being streams of living water, Introverted Churches more closely resemble stagnant pools. The percentage of congregants in the earliest (Exploring Christ) stage of spiritual growth in Introverted Churches is among the lowest of any of the church archetypes. Also, less than 7 percent of their congregants are newcomers to their church. Typically, the worship attendance at Introverted Churches has stayed the same or decreased over the past year. Reflecting their lack of outreach, their leaders are less likely than those of other church types to agree that the statement "We promote a strong serving culture that is widely recognized by the local community" accurately describes their church. With few newcomers or seekers, little community engagement, and a congregation uncomfortable with relational evangelism, Introverted Churches seem to have forgotten that the church exists for those who are not yet part of it.

6. An Uninspired, Traditional Approach to Ministry

Leaders of Introverted Churches choose *evangelical* as the best word to describe their church more often than leaders of other church archetypes. Likewise, they are less likely than others to choose *seeker-friendly* or *innovative*. These leaders see traditional ministries such as global outreach, children's ministry, men's ministry, and women's ministry as their signature church programs. Not surprisingly, they are less likely than pastors of other church types to say that evangelism training and local community outreach are signature programs.

7. Anychurch, USA

The Introverted Church archetype has few distinctive demographics. Their congregants don't stand out from other archetypes as being older or younger, more or less educated, higher or lower income, or more or less racially diverse. Introverted Churches are equally likely to be small or large; however, they are somewhat more likely than other church archetypes to be located in rural areas of the Midwest.

The following case study provides a classic example of an Introverted Church that accelerated its spiritual momentum in a big way—although Covenant Life Church didn't fit the classic profile at the time of its first REVEAL survey. In fact, most of its results were relatively "average." Nothing noteworthy stood out—until an unexpectedly high 15 percent of this older congregation of longtime churchgoers admitted that spiritually, they were "stalled." Then some of the more familiar signs of an Introverted Church culture emerged—such as below-average evangelism and serving numbers as well as a disappointingly low percentage that said they would "risk everything for Jesus Christ." A renovation of the heart was in order, which is exactly what the leaders of Covenant Life decided to tackle.

....

AN INTROVERTED-TO-ENERGIZED CASE STUDY:
COVENANT LIFE CHURCH, GRAND HAVEN, MICHIGAN

At its launch back in 1988, the promising future of Covenant Life Church may have seemed unlikely. It was founded when eight determined families—four from each of two Christian Reformed

TROUBLED

COMPLACENT

EXTROVERTED

AVERAGE

INTROVERTED

SELF-MOTIVATED

ENERGIZED

VIBRANT

Churches—opted to form their own tiny new congregation, believing there was a need for a different expression of ministry.

The church made its home in Grand Haven, a tourist-friendly town of about eleven thousand people located along Lake Michigan's eastern shore. But Covenant Life had no intention of just blending in to southwestern Michigan's church-on-every-corner environment. Instead, this fledgling congregation envisioned a less traditional style of worship and a greater emphasis on God's covenant (thus its name). And they were determined to be open and welcoming to everyone—including people who had failed and people who were hurting. Lead pastor Bruce Ballast says that more than twenty-five years later, this is still the case. "We have a lot of recovering alcoholics—and some not so recovering," he says. "We get referrals from a nearby pregnancy center and welcome those who have struggled with drug addiction." Today's congregation of more than 700 adults and 350 children is proactively inclusive.

As if to underscore its uniqueness, Covenant Life doesn't even look like a church. Nor does it want to. Instead, it has found its home in the historic former Story & Clark Piano Factory, which ceased operations in 1984. In 1994, Covenant Life carefully restored one of the century-old red brick, post-and-beam buildings into its Worship Center, although they intentionally retained the structure's concrete floors and furnished it with plastic chairs. "We've done nothing to fancy it up or make it look like a church," Bruce says. "So people who have been burned by a church or out of church for a long while, or who have rejected church for a variety of reasons—as well as those who have been here for a very long time—all feel at home."

And clearly, Bruce, along with discipleship pastor Bob DeVries, has not been content with maintaining the status quo when it comes to spiritual growth. Initially, Bob had served a dual role—as head of both operations and discipleship. But in mid-2009, he handed the operations responsibilities over to another staff member so he could focus solely on discipleship. "Bruce and I both felt a call to do a greater job in the discipleship of people," Bob explains, "and this led to a lot of discussions about what it really means to be a disciple of Jesus Christ."

As they progressed through that process, they increasingly heard about REVEAL from other area pastors. Bob read the first book about the survey[3] and says, "It just seemed to mirror so closely our own mission statement—and it gave us, for the first time, some language to really describe that with. So we proposed the survey to our elders."

The results of their initial November 2010 survey, including a Spiritual Vitality Index of 65, were disappointing. "We weren't real crazy about the words 'decidedly average,'" Bob recalls now, "but it gave us a place to start." He brought a team together—including elders, staff, and what he calls "some very smart people"—to process the results. "We've got an amazing group to work with here—people who are really fired up about the vision of living it out and being true to our mission," he says. "And Bruce is very strategically driven, so he keeps us focused and moving forward." This leadership group responded to their "decidedly average" profile with two key decisions.

Leadership Decision #1 was to find ways to make "spiritual growth" come to life.

Despite being part of a very "churched" community, the REVEAL survey clearly showed that most of Covenant Life's congregants were either Exploring Christ or Growing in Christ.[4] This reaffirmed and reinvigorated the church leaders' objective of discipleship, leading them to develop what Bob describes as "some fairly specific initiatives" toward spiritual growth. This included various hands-on

[3] Greg L. Hawkins and Cally Parkinson, *REVEAL: Where Are You?* (South Barrington, IL: Willow Creek Association, 2007).
[4] Typically, the majority of congregants in Introverted Churches are in the Close to Christ and Christ-Centered stages of growth, with very few in the Exploring Christ segment. As in the case of CLC, this norm does not hold true for all Introverted Churches.

TROUBLED

COMPLACENT

EXTROVERTED

AVERAGE

INTROVERTED

SELF-MOTIVATED

ENERGIZED

VIBRANT

"tools"—resources and opportunities specifically designed to build bridges to the next levels of spiritual maturity.

One of these tools was a *literal* bridge. Constructed in an on-site woodshop by men's ministry craftsmen (who more typically build ramps for wheelchair users and beds for children who need them), the wooden bridge represents the three movements between REVEAL's four spiritual segments. As people walk across this twenty-four-foot–long structure, they can read the catalysts that contribute to each spiritual transition, engraved right into the wood itself. "We keep this in our Main Street area, which people walk through before going into our Worship Center or into our coffee shop where we project the services," Bob says. "We've also incorporated it into several different sermon series as a way to bring home what it means to grow spiritually."

Not all their new "tools" have been quite so visible. Covenant Life redid its introduction of the church to visitors with its "Discover CLC" class, including a discussion of spiritual growth as well as Covenant Life's mission and vision. They incorporated similar discussions into their new member classes, bringing home the idea that all attenders are on a journey. They even revamped their weekly bulletin, making it very light on announcements so the entire interior remained available for sermon notes as well as the teaching pastor's suggestions for extending that day's message into the week ahead.

Have attenders responded to these and other resources now at their disposal? Indeed they have. "What's been very gratifying to Bruce and to me," Bob says, "is that the more we provide tools for people to grow in their faith, the more they use them."

Leadership Decision #2 was to vigorously encourage personal spiritual practices.

While these new tools helped set the stage for spiritual growth, it was Covenant Life's renewed focus on spiritual practices that was most instrumental in moving congregants toward increased levels of maturity—starting with a multifaceted immersion in Scripture.

Covenant Life Embedded the Bible—
Beginning with an Eighteen-Month Deep Dive into Scripture

In September 2011, Bruce and Bob launched an eighteen-month sermon series ranging from the Old Testament up through Jesus' ministry, using an existing template but writing all their own messages. They occasionally inserted a shorter series that highlighted a particular spiritual discipline, among them an especially powerful seven-week series on prayer. They also developed a Bible-reading plan for each week, which included an all-church memory verse, as well as a section called Live It, to encourage congregants to integrate what they were learning into their daily lives.

In addition, leaders took a serious look at the church's small group ministry, in light of REVEAL's conclusion that this is especially important to those in the Exploring or Growing segments of spiritual maturity. "We redefined our groups a bit," Bob explains, "to a small group being any place where faith-building community is happening." So—beyond providing Bible reading plans for the entire congregation—the church leaders also created related materials for small groups. In January 2014, they replicated much of this effort when they launched an eight-week series on the New Testament. In those eight weeks, the congregation read the entire New Testament and met in small groups weekly as they took on "The New Testament Challenge."

If you think all of this sounds like a whole lot of work, you would be right. And Bruce and Bob admit that this thought has occurred to them. "You know, we've asked each other a couple different times, 'Man, you write a sermon and then it's small group material and then it's something for the inside of the bulletin and then it's the Bible-reading plan. Like, holy cow, what have we done to ourselves?'"

But as they share this, they are laughing. And they are eager to add that the work is definitely worth it. When Covenant Life celebrated its twenty-fifth anniversary as a church, various pastors visited with messages for the congregation—leaving Bruce and Bob without their typical weekly assignments. "And actually, during this time, it was really kind of nice to hear from a number of people, 'Hey, where's the small group stuff?' or 'Where's our Bible-reading plan? What's going on?'" Bob says. "So we know people are actually looking for it and using it."

Covenant Life Pastored the Community—by Letting the Spirit Move

As Covenant Life has thrived, the larger community has taken notice, often asking what accounts for the church's growth. In June 2013, Bruce wrote a three-page letter in response to one such inquiry, citing various factors and quoting leaders from John Maxwell and Andy Stanley to Peter Wagner, a church-growth expert from a previous generation. Bruce covered several topics, but his longest and most heartfelt explanation centered on "an utter dependence on the power of the Spirit." He wrote, "The additional ingredient you will find in a growing church is an active, passionate, involved prayer ministry. And . . . a sense of humility that acknowledges nothing is going to happen unless God causes it, and therefore he gets all the glory."

Which is the reason that when it comes to Covenant Life's service to the larger community, nothing is automatically off the table. Everything is prayerfully considered. And the results can take off in ways never imagined.

"In the last couple of years, we have seen the Spirit just breaking out in some surprising ways," says Bruce. Take the men's ministry, for instance, mentioned earlier for their bridge, bed, and wheelchair ramp building. Many of these men are responding to the church's spiritual growth challenge in unexpected ways. For example, some have stepped up to shopping—*grocery* shopping. "On Thursday nights they go buy food and just drop it off anonymously to people in need they've heard about through a variety of sources," Bruce explains. "Then some of them go serve meals at a homeless shelter. Things just happen that we didn't plan, because people are trying to live out their faith—and we're now in the stage of trying to encourage that."

Covenant Life members mentor at-risk students in their local elementary school, they have expanded their DivorceCare ministry to include programs for the children of broken families, and they have opened up their building for use by the community. In fact, on Thursday mornings, they inflate several bounce houses, brew lots of coffee, and, through the local paper, invite moms, dads, and their kids to "Bounce Around"—a couple of hours of play and fellowship for the general community. "It's a free, safe, nice environment for people to come and have conversation and experience community," Bob explains. "It's amazing how God has used that."

Bruce sums up Covenant Life's service initiatives by saying they're a combination of spontaneity and planning. "We're all so open to see the Spirit moving and to see people wanting to serve," he says. "We're not about to say, 'Hey, that's not part of the plan. You can't do that.'"

✛   ✛   ✛

Interestingly, the three-page letter Bruce wrote to explain his church's growth was to a leader in the Christian Reformed Church—the denomination that supported this fledgling church until it organized in 1996. While Bruce and Bob acknowledge that their church is far from typical within the denomination, they agree that the denomination has valuable insights to share—including its solid teaching relating to today's world and time-tested wisdom that makes it unnecessary for the church to reinvent the wheel when it faces new situations. Covenant Life also has much to contribute, grounded in its progress documented in its second REVEAL survey, taken in

November 2012. The percentages of congregants in the two initial spiritual segments (Exploring and Growing) declined as people matured, for instance, sending the Close to Christ category up from 25 to 32 percent. The number of people who had described themselves as "stalled" or "dissatisfied" declined by more than 50 percent. Every single personal spiritual practice surged ahead, and their Spiritual Vitality Index rose from 65 to 73.

But numbers can't tell the whole story. What, Bob is asked, do people say has changed? What makes them eager to join in? "The most common comment we get from people," he answers, "is that we want to help people grow. That they feel challenged to grow."

Gratifying responses indeed for a church determined to honor its namesake covenant from God by listening to the Spirit and following through with an intentional focus on achieving discipleship.

THE HOPE FOR THE INTROVERTED CHURCH

The desire to reach any destination craves a path. Whether that desire is to hike up a mountain to see the world from its peak or to stand at the Olympic Games as a medal-winning athlete, the journey begins with a search for next steps.

The spiritual journey leading to a relationship with Christ seems to prompt this same desire. Or stated differently, multiple conversations with REVEAL church leaders confirm that spiritual momentum accelerates when a plan for growth is clearly defined—when its different stages are identified and the catalysts of progress in each stage are described with some precision.

This is particularly true for an Introverted Church, as demonstrated in a surprisingly concrete way by Covenant Life. Building a physical replica of the spiritual path (like their bridge) is certainly not essential, but Introverted congregations (as well as others) benefit greatly when a church defines a clear spiritual framework that identifies the different stages of development—then provides resources that address the needs of each stage.

Covenant Life used the REVEAL Spiritual Continuum to define and communicate its growth plan. Many churches have pursued a similar strategy, though others preferred creating their own version of a path that leads to increasing intimacy with Christ. For example, you may recall that the Extroverted Church case study in chapter 4 described Grace Community's decision to simplify and focus its discipleship strategy on one word: *relationship*. Then the Average Church case study in chapter 5 described Legacy Church's adoption, with substantive modification, of the REVEAL Spiritual Continuum. Clearly, evidence compiled by REVEAL to date shows that providing a spiritual growth framework that people can grasp bears great fruit.

This works because a pathway defines expectations and prerequisites for progress. Think about the Introverted Church congregants. They are believers who are committed to the values of the Christian faith. But they seem to be unclear about how to live out that faith in their daily lives—which may explain why satisfaction with the church's role is often somewhat low. While pastors may be reluctant to offer a defined spiritual path—possibly because it suggests that an achievable destination exists—its absence leaves new and even mature believers rudderless. To be clear, these frameworks for growth are less about how to "do" faith (for example, get in a small group, serve the poor, read the Bible) than how to "be" faithful. Chapter 10 expands on how to inspire people to "be" more like Christ, with additional practical next steps for the Introverted Church.

COVENANT LIFE CHURCH: 2014 UPDATE

What's the single biggest difference in Covenant Life Church since the case study?

Covenant Life reports a surge in the desire for spiritual growth, based on significant increases in small group participation, men's and

TROUBLED

COMPLACENT

EXTROVERTED

AVERAGE

INTROVERTED

SELF-MOTIVATED

ENERGIZED

VIBRANT

Symptoms of an Introverted Church

A church likely falls into the Introverted Church archetype if these three primary characteristics are present:

1. *Congregants are spiritually mature, but more Mary than Martha.* Beliefs are solid and spiritual practices are commonplace. But congregant conversations rarely turn to stories about reaching nonbelievers or local serving experiences, and leaders suspect those occasions are sporadic at best.
2. *Leaders detect signs of spiritual stagnation.* Newcomers are few and far between, little relational evangelism or community outreach is occurring, and the church culture may be becoming more clannish with less openness and tolerance for outsiders.
3. *Congregants show signs of unrest.* Dissatisfaction with the church may be high, but its root is in misplaced expectations. The church may be communicating that they are the one-stop shop for all things needed for congregants' spiritual journeys, rather than helping their people take ownership of their spiritual growth and view the church as one resource among many.

women's group activities, and volunteers across the board. According to Discipleship Pastor Bob DeVries, the spiritual temperature is definitely up.

What's new in Covenant Life's discipleship strategies and culture since the case study?

Bob credits the New Testament Challenge, modeled after Biblica's Community Bible Experience, with helping people "fall in love with God's Word again." For eight weeks in early 2014, participants read ten pages of Scripture daily and met weekly in small groups for a "book club" study experience. Leading up to Easter, they pursued a slower, deeper study about the "Living Power of the Resurrection," reinforcing the themes of reflection and meditation in reading plans and small group material.

The congregation also embraced a community-service initiative called Special Treasures, supporting families with children, and especially adolescents, with special needs. The church's tradesmen built facilities to provide after-school care for kids with varying degrees of developmental challenges, including autism. Students in this after-school program—called Regatta—recently led worship in a very powerful service.

What's next on the horizon for Covenant Life Church?

Providing a clearer discipleship pathway is the top priority, with a special focus on individuals at each end of the Spiritual Continuum. For those at the very beginning of their journey, the church wants to develop a "first step" similar to Alpha or Starting Point. For those who are more spiritually mature, Covenant Life's leaders plan to implement a discipleship approach called Core Four that encourages those who want "more than small groups" to experiment with the greater accountability and spiritual depth offered by a group of three or four people.

TROUBLED

COMPLACENT

EXTROVERTED

AVERAGE

INTROVERTED

SELF-MOTIVATED

ENERGIZED

VIBRANT

TROUBLED

COMPLACENT

EXTROVERTED

AVERAGE

INTROVERTED

SELF-MOTIVATED

ENERGIZED

VIBRANT

CHAPTER 7
THE SELF-MOTIVATED CHURCH

The "empty nest" is a myth. While children do transition from first steps to first dates to first jobs—and finally to a physical departure from home—they never fully sever their emotional dependence on parental love and acceptance. One of the greatest challenges for parents is to navigate this evolution from a micromanaging role of vetting playmates and enforcing curfews to a relationship of influence and mutual respect.

The emotional and relational issues that complicate this transition are the very ones that confound and confront the Self-Motivated Church.

Self-Motivated congregations are everything the name implies—spiritually energetic, mature followers of Christ who are positive and confident about their faith, prepared to face and overcome whatever setbacks block their path. They do not depend on the church for prodding or supervision because all the motivation they need is already embedded in their minds and hearts through their deep connection and intimacy with God.

This sounds like a pastor's dream congregation, doesn't it? A Self-Motivated church in Calgary, Canada, would beg to differ. On their third round of REVEAL surveys, their composite SVI (from their more than one-thousand-member congregation attending three campuses) has yet to budge much beyond a very average score of 70. Yet there's significant evidence of accelerating spiritual momentum. For example, the two most mature segments—Close to Christ and Christ-Centered— have increased from a collective 50 percent to 65 percent. More than one out of four say they reflect on Scripture for "meaning in my life" every day, which is well above the REVEAL norm. And small groups are posting much higher satisfaction rates, possibly due to campaigns such as "40 Days in the Word," that have integrated small group curriculum and weekend services. Evangelism activity and connections with spiritual friends have shown impressive gains as well.

Yet satisfaction with the church declined from 58 percent to 52 percent, which—although still "average" by REVEAL standards—is surprisingly low given the advances reported for so many spiritual markers. It is this halfhearted approval of the church's role in spiritual growth that drags down its SVI. Imagine the confusion of the pastors when they saw data testifying to a rising spiritual temperature alongside facts indicating congregational discontent. It seems illogical. Counterintuitive. Frustrating.

A clue to what's afoot emerges from the top concerns reported by the most dissatisfied congregants. According to this list, the church's primary deficiency is in its efforts to "help me feel like I belong." Does this mean people have trouble making connections, such as getting into small groups? More likely, it is the reaction of a maturing congregation struggling to adapt as the church dedicates increasing attention to expanding regional sites. Similar to children who feel displaced when parents are distracted by attention-grabbing issues—like a job change or a dying relative—Self-Motivated congregants seem to yearn for reassurance that the church loves and appreciates them and continues to be devoted to their spiritual growth. They may sense that the church has turned aside, moved on to "greener pastures" since discipleship progress seems to be perking along—causing them to feel less and less like "I belong."

These circumstances were clearly evident in a Self-Motivated Church in Texas, located in the fastest-growing county in the country. Sandwiched between a large Sun City retirement community and a residential development that will grow to include three thousand new homes, the pastors see the potential for explosive growth. But their very mature congregants (70 percent fell in the Close to Christ and Christ-Centered categories) are unhappy campers. Based on their REVEAL results, satisfaction with the church *and* with the senior pastor was just 43 percent, well below average, and—like the Canadian church—contributed to an unremarkable SVI of 70 despite very impressive spiritual measures.

This disaffection for the church may be partially due to the recent amicable parting with the senior pastor, who has yet to be replaced. It may also be due to recent experiments with a contemporary service, since worship showed up as a "hot button" issue for weekend services. However, the top concern for the most dissatisfied congregants was neither worship nor leadership. Their number one request for the church was to "provide a clear pathway to guide growth" (which is often cited as the greatest need by mature but dissatisfied congregants in the REVEAL database).

The executive pastor admitted that a discipleship pathway "has not been communicated clearly." They are preparing to launch a discipleship plan this fall, he explains, one designed to work with different forms of media to appeal to younger people. Their Self-Motivated congregation will likely embrace this strategy—but *not* necessarily because the spiritually thriving congregants need a discipleship plan. Rather, it may appeal to them because they seem impatient with their church—frustrated by its inattention to discipleship, which is a by-product of other distractions.

The Achilles' heel of the Self-Motivated Church is derived from its

TROUBLED

COMPLACENT

EXTROVERTED

AVERAGE

INTROVERTED

SELF-MOTIVATED

ENERGIZED

VIBRANT

greatest strength, which is the spiritual maturity of its people. Church leaders who see their people so clearly on the right track may feel released from the need to nurture their spiritual development. It's not surprising that pastors would naturally turn their attention and the majority of church resources to drawing in and growing up newcomers who are fresh to the faith. But if not done carefully, that can be a mistake.

Returning to the parenting analogy sheds light on why this may be true. Making the transition from the command-and-control parenting style that works for toddlers to a relationship defined by influence and advice—which is so essential for young adults—is tricky. But good parents do not stop being parents because their twenty-five-year-old has assembled the basic building blocks of life and is financially independent. Good parents may take a backseat, but they continue to inspire, motivate, cheer the successes, and lament the failures as their young adult children make decisions that shape the kind of impact they can have in this world. Good parents do not do this out of obligation—because their "official" obligations to their children are complete. They inspire, motivate, cheer on, and lament with their grown-up offspring out of love.

This is the opportunity for the Self-Motivated Church—to transition from being a spiritual "parent" who turns away when obligations seem complete, to a spiritual "cheerleader" who provides continuing encouragement and support out of love. This shift may take some leadership soul-searching, and it will admittedly be difficult to accomplish—but just as good parents can make it happen, so, too, can the Self-Motivated Church.

SIX FACTORS THAT SET THE SELF-MOTIVATED CHURCH APART

1. High Frequency Spirituality

The levels of core Christian beliefs, engagement in personal spiritual practices, and faith in action at Self-Motivated Churches are very high—and quite similar to those of Vibrant Churches, as shown in Chart 7.1. A high percentage of congregants in Self-Motivated Churches are serving, tithing, sharing their faith, and spending time in prayer and reflecting on Scripture. In fact, their rates of engaging in these behaviors exceed the database average by 20 to 40 percent. Self-Motivated Churches have the highest percentage of Christ-Centered congregants, with about one-third of the congregation in this most-mature segment of spiritual growth, compared to just 5 percent in the Exploring Christ segment.

2. Unrealized Expectations

Self-Motivated Churches differ from Vibrant Churches in congregants' feelings about their church's role in their spiritual growth. As shown in Chart 7.2, Self-Motivated congregants express middling levels of satisfaction with four of the five Best Practice Principles. Their satisfaction with their senior pastor is also about 10 percent

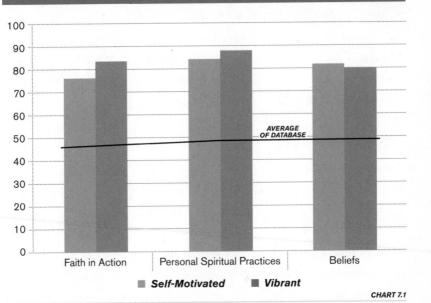

CONGREGANTS IN SELF-MOTIVATED CHURCHES ARE HIGHLY ENGAGED

AVERAGE OF DATABASE

Faith in Action   Personal Spiritual Practices   Beliefs

■ *Self-Motivated*   ■ *Vibrant*

CHART 7.1

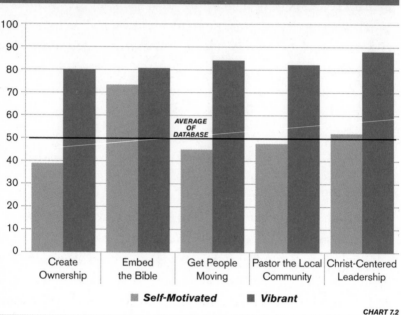

SATISFACTION IS UNREMARKABLE IN A SELF-MOTIVATED CHURCH

AVERAGE OF DATABASE

Create Ownership | Embed the Bible | Get People Moving | Pastor the Local Community | Christ-Centered Leadership

■ *Self-Motivated*   ■ *Vibrant*

CHART 7.2

below the average for all church types. It is difficult to know if congregants in Self-Motivated Churches are holding their church to a higher standard due to the intensity of their own efforts to grow spiritually, or if these churches truly are not doing much to promote spiritual growth. Either way, it is clear that congregants in Self-Motivated Churches expect more from their church.

3. Servants at Heart

Congregants of Self-Motivated Churches are highly engaged in serving others. Forty percent serve in a ministry at their church on a weekly basis—the highest percentage of any archetype. Twenty-nine percent serve those in need through their church once a month or more. A larger number, 43 percent, serve those in need at least once a month on their own. Undergirding their service is a strong belief that they are called by God to be involved in the lives of the poor and suffering. Congregants of Self-Motivated Churches very strongly agree with this belief, at a rate that is 20 percent above the database average. They also very strongly agree with the statement "I know and use my spiritual gifts to fulfill God's purposes" at a higher rate than all but Vibrant Church congregants.

4. Vanishing Congregants

While a high percentage of Self-Motivated churchgoers have attended their church for the past ten years or longer, their lack of satisfaction may be prompting them to look elsewhere to find a better environment for growth. We see this tendency expressed in shrinking attendance in Self-Motivated Churches, which are more likely than other archetypes to report that their weekend attendance has been on a downward trend over the past twelve months. They also are somewhat more likely to be smaller congregations to start with, so declines in attendance can be especially troublesome.

5. Large-Group Ministry Strategy

When asked to name the distinctive or signature programs of their church, leaders of Self-Motivated Churches tend to say that they major in large-group options such as men's and women's ministries. Compared to leaders of other archetypes, they also are more likely to say that adult Sunday school classes are among their distinctives, and they are less likely to mention small groups.

6. Older, Rural Southern Congregations

Self-Motivated Churches are more often found in the south-central states (Texas, Arkansas, Oklahoma, and Louisiana) and in the Southeast. They are more likely to be located in rural communities. Compared to other church types, congregants attending Self-Motivated Churches are more likely to be age fifty-five or older and less likely to have a college degree.

TROUBLED

COMPLACENT

EXTROVERTED

AVERAGE

INTROVERTED

SELF-MOTIVATED

ENERGIZED

VIBRANT

The following case study describes a Self-Motivated Church that exhibits most of the archetype's classic characteristics. The combination of its remarkable profile of spiritual maturity with its dismal satisfaction ratings in the initial survey meant that Warm Beach Free Methodist Church faced a tough audience—including a number of retired pastors from within its denomination. While not quite breaking through to the Vibrant Church archetype, Warm Beach made tremendous gains by reengaging their disillusioned Christ followers in the strategy and the story of their church.

A SELF-MOTIVATED CASE STUDY:
WARM BEACH FREE METHODIST CHURCH, STANWOOD, WASHINGTON

To fully appreciate the progress achieved by the Warm Beach Free Methodist Church, you may need to set aside some preconceived notions. For starters, forget about walking barefoot in the sand: Located fifty miles north of Seattle, Warm Beach inhabits the cold, wet environs of Puget Sound—where its across-the-road neighbors include the state's largest Christian campground and a retirement center catering to former pastors. The three-hundred-member congregation's two pastors are incredibly single-minded in their vision and mutual support—despite their three-decade age difference. And when launching its spiritual growth initiatives, the church did so in reverse order—first addressing the further growth of its most mature Christians.

Senior pastor Pat Vance, who has served at Warm Beach for the past twenty of the church's forty-seven years, has long sought input from those he serves and worked to accommodate their needs. Associate pastor Sam Schaar arrived at Warm Beach as an intern in 2010, upon completion of his graduate work at Princeton Theological Seminary. He, too, was eager to pursue new initiatives. By the time

the internship ended, he and Pat knew they would make good partners in leading Warm Beach forward.

One of their mutual concerns was that there were too few opportunities for congregants—most of whom were middle-aged and
longtime Christians—to go deeper in their faith. Pat was dissatisfied
with the church's fragmented approach to classes, including leadership training. "I kept thinking I'd like to do it all in one place," he
explains. "So I got the ball rolling, and Sam really grabbed it."

"We felt like we had spread ourselves too thin, trying to do things
in all different places," Sam agrees. With a passion for ministry based
on in-depth discipleship and teaching, he adds, "I yearned to see all
those things kind of done in one place and done at a level that was
deeper and that offered an opportunity for people to commit to
something that was going to stretch them pretty significantly."

As a result, planning began in earnest on an initiative called
Disciple Road—a school-year–long program of weekly two-hour
classes that would be divided into three quarterly segments limited
to twenty people, and described as so demanding that participants
might well have to give up other activities in Disciple Road's favor.

Pulling this initiative together was also demanding, requiring two
full years for church leaders to complete. Then, as this process moved
toward conclusion, a nearby Free Methodist Church recommended
the REVEAL survey. "They said it was really helpful to them," Pat
says, "because it got at how their people were doing spiritually."

As a result, Warm Beach congregants took their first REVEAL survey in the spring of 2012, a few months before the scheduled launch
of Disciple Road. And while their survey results were clear and compelling, they also seemed counterintuitive. Here were congregation
members of obvious spiritual maturity (two-thirds of them residing
in either the Close to Christ or Christ-Centered segments) who professed an unmet need for greater spiritual depth. Here was a church
filled with people demonstrating well-above-average core beliefs and

TROUBLED

COMPLACENT

EXTROVERTED

AVERAGE

INTROVERTED

SELF-MOTIVATED

ENERGIZED

VIBRANT

personal spiritual practices who were, however, less than satisfied with their church and, in particular, their church's weekend services.

In short, through the survey Warm Beach congregants told their church they needed greater support for their already well-established faith in Jesus Christ.

Pat and Sam were neither surprised nor upset by these results; in fact, their own insights—and their two-year planning response to those insights—were affirmed. "I kind of saw that as a window on the fact that you can't just do church from week to week the sort of traditional way and expect much spiritual depth," Pat says. "It said to me that programs alone don't do it."

Leadership Decision #1 was to move full speed ahead with the launch of Disciple Road.

Fifteen congregants signed up for the initial September-through-May sessions, ready to devote approximately three months each to three modules: "Who Has God Made Me to Be?," "Who Is God?," and What Does God Want Me to Do?

Often asked why "Who Is God?" is not the lead topic, Sam explains that the choice was deliberate, and a nod to those participants who are fairly new to faith. "This module is kind of an orientation to where you've been and who you are right now," he says. "It gives people some touch points to work with and a way to orient themselves to what is ahead." Various activities contribute to that goal, including each individual's composition of a spiritual biography describing the role—or lack of one—that faith had played in his or her life to that point. Along with such self-discovery tools as a spiritual gifts inventory, the StrengthsFinder test, and the Myers-Briggs personality inventory, the group reads *Sacred Rhythms*, a book on spiritual growth by Ruth Haley Barton.

Discussion of "Who Is God?," the most extensive of the three modules, began after Christmas with two weeks spent on church history, two more on an orientation to Scripture, and then eight weeks on theology and Scripture itself. The group reads and discusses *An Exploration of Christian Theology* by Don Thorsen, an ambitious undertaking. "This is the demanding module in terms of homework and discussion," Sam says, acknowledging that the two-hour sessions on doctrine and theology often continue well beyond their dismissal time.

After a short break, students regroup for "What Does God Want Me to Do?," which focuses on topics like active listening, pastoral care, mentoring, coaching, and ways each person can use the spiritual gifts they identified in module 1. The group reads *Strengthening the Soul of Your Leadership*, also by Ruth Haley Barton, and takes a one-day off-site retreat during which each person prays and listens for God's guidance—sometimes with some very profound results.

Leadership Decision #2 was to leverage Pat and Sam's multigenerational partnership.

Now in its second year, Disciple Road is but one example of how Warm Beach's sixty-two-year-old pastor and his thirty-year-old counterpart combine their interests and talents to encourage greater spiritual depth. "One of the things people love about our church is its generational diversity," Pat says. "They love Sam, and they're also glad to have the older guy in the front office." Between the two of them, Pat and Sam encourage and appeal to every part of their congregation—from senior adults to preschoolers, active in everything from weekend services to a wide range of midweek opportunities. (Before each Wednesday evening service, for instance, the whole congregation enjoys dinner together.)

The two pastors' partnership was particularly on display during a recent sermon series, in which they initially set out to unpack the church's tagline: "Warm Beach Free Methodist Church—Teaching the Way of Jesus Christ for Wholeness and Mission." Rather than one pastor taking the lead or each of them standing behind the pulpit every other week, they did each service together—seated at a barista table in front of a coffeehouse setting, sipping coffee as they talked. The original three-month plan turned into a year of conversations, covering topics including the parables, the Sermon on the Mount, and spiritual formation—always with one pastor leading the weekly discussion, but with frequent, and sometimes extemporaneous, interaction between them. What they were teaching was designed to deepen the congregation's faith, and the unique way they did it made this memorable teaching especially impactful.

+   +   +

It was in the midst of these conversational weekend messages that Warm Beach congregants took their second REVEAL survey, one that would affirm the church's enhanced emphasis on spiritual depth and multigenerational support. The church, which continued to fit within the Self-Motivated archetype, saw its Spiritual Vitality Index (SVI) rise dramatically, from 70 to 79.[1] Already-high numbers in spiritual beliefs climbed even further (belief in the Trinity went from 84 percent to 94 percent, for instance, and belief in the authority of the Bible rose from 52 percent to 67 percent). Spiritual practices increased as well, including daily reflection on Scripture from 31 percent to 35 percent, Bible reading from 34 percent to 40 percent, and prayer for guidance from 58 percent to 71 percent.

But it was the Warm Beach congregation's obvious satisfaction with their church's new faith-deepening emphasis that was truly off the charts. Satisfaction rose when it came to weekend services (from 43 to 61 percent), the church (from 32 to 60 percent), and the senior pastor (from 58 to 75 percent). By the same token, previous negatives dropped dramatically, in areas from dissatisfaction with the church

---

[1] This increase moves Warm Beach from an SVI that is at the database average to one that is in the top 25 percent of churches. Despite such a significant gain, Warm Beach did not shift into the Vibrant Church archetype because these churches score in the top 5 percent of the database and have much higher levels of satisfaction with the Best Practice Principles.

(from 34 to 15 percent) to congregants considering leaving the church (from 11 to 6 percent). Now Warm Beach's overall congregational satisfaction with the church was newly aligned with individual Warm Beach congregants' ever-deepening spiritual growth.

Such results are directly traceable to Warm Beach's deliberate strategies in the year between their two surveys. Remember that Disciple Road had been in the planning stages for two years before the first survey was taken, so the work that had gone into that initiative also played a role in implementing each of the following strategies:

Warm Beach Got Their People Moving—by Moving in Reverse Order

Once the demanding and faith-deepening Disciple Road course was available to their church's Christians, Warm Beach designed and implemented two more courses: Next Step and then, First Step. "We were in the second year of Disciple Road," Pat explains, "and I said to Sam, 'Okay, so we're giving them what they need, but we've got new people coming in who aren't ready for that. And we still have a membership issue to deal with. How do we handle that?'" The pastors' solution was to launch fall and spring Next Step luncheons, during which church leaders describe the church, answer questions, hand out packets of information, and follow up with individual conversations.

With Disciple Road and Next Step in place, Pat says he and Sam went backward once again. "I got personally convicted about continuing to invite people to receive Christ," he says. "So we put together First Step, specifically for those who were actively looking into Christianity. Sam designed this very simple, really nice three-month program for those who accept Christ, lining them up with a mentor—often a Disciple Road grad—to go through the book of John."

Warm Beach Created Ownership—Through Storytelling

Participants in these classes, as well as in other church initiatives, are encouraged to share their stories with the congregation. Pat

TROUBLED

COMPLACENT

EXTROVERTED

AVERAGE

INTROVERTED

SELF-MOTIVATED

ENERGIZED

VIBRANT

remembers, for instance, the story told by a recent widow who prayed for guidance during her Disciple Road silent retreat. She continuously asked God for her next step, and came away with the word *children*. At the time, she told the church, she had no idea what that could mean. But today she oversees the childcare responsibilities for the church's thriving MOPS (Moms of Preschoolers) program.

Such story sharing has made a significant difference to everyone, not just to those participating in Disciple Road, First Step, or Next Step. The mere fact that these faith-deepening opportunities are available—and that stories of their results are widely shared—uplifts the entire congregation.

Warm Beach Embedded the Bible—Through Teaching and Beyond

"I think what was verified for us in the survey is that people expect good, Bible-based content," Pat says. "You know, I'm always amazed when people come up after they visit our church and say, 'Thank you so much for preaching out of the Bible.' Well, you know—hello? What are we supposed to be doing?" And if visitors appreciate Bible teaching, Warm Beach's congregation demands it. "We serve meat and potatoes and we even stretch our people, but we have fun doing it," Pat adds.

That Bible-based enjoyment shows up in many directions: in major missions participation from Bolivia to India; in extremely well-attended Sunday school classes and small groups; in higher-than-average stewardship and serving. (And speaking of meat and potatoes, on the fifth Sunday of any month that has one, the whole congregation gathers for lunch following a single weekend service. Another prayer, storytelling, and class information opportunity, we're sure.)

So who cares if Warm Beach's beachfront location is on the cool side? Their hearts are obviously warm for one another. And when it comes to their faith and their love of Jesus, they're on fire.

THE HOPE FOR THE SELF-MOTIVATED CHURCH

The idea of measuring congregant satisfaction is difficult for many church leaders to accept. Even high satisfaction marks can make leaders squirm, struggling perhaps with the notion that allowing such a "consumerist" approach to guide strategies and decisions conflicts with the church's divine mission.

But REVEAL church clients have found satisfaction results to be surprisingly powerful lenses for understanding what might ignite spiritual momentum. That's because satisfaction with the church—and especially satisfaction with the senior pastor—defines its "platform of permission," which means it serves as a benchmark for the love and respect people have for the church, and how willing they are to follow its leaders. In other words, a church with high satisfaction—one with a strong "platform of permission"—can introduce even radical changes with confidence, knowing their congregants will embrace whatever new initiatives are introduced. Churches with lower satisfaction, like the Self-Motivated Church, don't have that luxury. They don't have that "permission."

The hope for the Self-Motivated Church is that the first step toward strengthening their "platform of permission" is to do something that's relatively painless, even easy. It doesn't require a lot of soul-searching or a massive ministry overhaul. In fact, every Self-Motivated Church in the REVEAL database *has already taken* this step. Which, simply put, is to listen.

Ask any parent who has helped steer a self-indulgent adolescent into self-reliant adulthood about their most effective strategy, and the answer will likely relate to listening. The hope for the Self-Motivated Church is to go down this same path—which means to ask for the unvarnished truth about what's going on in its people's spiritual lives and for unfiltered feedback about what the church can do to help them.

Could this be taken as a plug for doing the REVEAL survey?

TROUBLED

COMPLACENT

EXTROVERTED

AVERAGE

INTROVERTED

SELF-MOTIVATED

ENERGIZED

VIBRANT

Symptoms of a Self-Motivated Church

A church likely falls into the Self-Motivated Church archetype if these three primary characteristics exist:

1. *Pastors are confident that the majority of congregants are living out their faith.* It's hard to miss the spiritual energy radiating from congregational interactions and activity. Biblical literacy is clearly high. Serving opportunities are very popular. Congregants are eager to fill whatever needs surface in the church or community.

2. *Pastors perceive a sense of disenchantment with the church that may be growing.* There's almost a feeling of estrangement affecting the relationship of church leaders with the congregation. It's possible that congregants suspect that their leaders are preoccupied with efforts to appeal to newcomers, creating a ripple of disappointment—even resentment—that may be infecting church culture.

3. *Attendance is declining, often despite leadership moves to reverse the trend.* Attrition is taking a toll on attendance at the same time newcomers are stable or dwindling. It's likely that church leaders have attempted to create a friendlier atmosphere, or open new campuses, or experiment with different worship styles to attract higher numbers to attend services. But such efforts can easily backfire.

Maybe. But it's more of an encouragement for church leaders to do *whatever it takes* to get a fresh, honest perspective on the spiritual needs of their people. The Self-Motivated Church faces a unique dilemma, which is a spiritually mature congregation at odds with their church. These veteran followers of Christ don't want to be told what they need, or to be ignored. They want to be heard. And the Self-Motivated Church would do well to listen to them—because their hearts and voices already belong to Jesus.

WARM BEACH FREE METHODIST CHURCH: 2014 UPDATE

What's the single biggest difference in Warm Beach Church since the case study?

Warm Beach finished their second Disciple Road cohort in May 2014, one year after their second REVEAL survey. The act of recognizing and hearing testimony from this second round of "graduates" reinforced the power of this intense discipleship experience. Pastor Sam Schaar tells the story of a handyman who discerned that craftsmanship is his spiritual gift as well as his job—and that his workplace is his mission field, where he now regularly prays with coworkers. His cohort included a woman in her seventies and two high school seniors. Per Sam, Disciple Road's curriculum is intentionally set at a tenth-grade reading level, offering a spiritually enriching opportunity for adolescent congregants as well as adults.

What's new in Warm Beach's discipleship strategies and culture since the case study?

Most immediately, while senior pastor Pat is on a three-month sabbatical, the church is engaged in a "Sabbatical Summer." The traditional Sunday school is suspended until the fall, and the church has merged its two services and children's programs into a single 10:00 a.m. Sunday service that *everyone* attends followed by an all-inclusive fellowship gathering. Children are equipped with activity packets customized to help them engage with the rest of their friends and family in the weekend message. The intent is to activate the multigenerational relationship modeled by Sam and Pat across the church.

What's next on the horizon for Warm Beach Free Methodist Church?

Warm Beach will launch its third Disciple Road cohort in the fall, and Sam hopes to be able to integrate a number of people from their youth ministries into the process. They also plan to dive deeply into an inquiry about how to talk about spiritual formation with their congregants, with an intention, Sam says, to reinforce a budding "mega-shift from doing to being."

CHAPTER 8

THE ENERGIZED CHURCH

TROUBLED

COMPLACENT

EXTROVERTED

AVERAGE

INTROVERTED

SELF-MOTIVATED

ENERGIZED

VIBRANT

Goals. Lists. Ministry Vision. Strategic Plans. This is the Energized Church. Focused, well led, and much appreciated by its growing congregations, the Energized Church is a beacon of spiritual activity—and that activity is rarely haphazard. It is carefully designed to promote the spiritual development of its congregants by using a menu of options to address the needs of varying levels of spiritual maturity.

Two recent conversations with Energized Churches highlight the intentional nature of this archetype's discipleship agenda. First, a Presbyterian church in an affluent Denver suburb described in detail the massive transition underway in its small group system—which was "in ruins" when the current pastor arrived on the scene four years earlier. At that time, small groups were decentralized, with a loosely defined goal of providing fellowship. Now, however, they form the discipleship engine of the church, charged with delivering a spiritual experience composed of seven key elements including prayer, service, mission, gifts, and body life (an appropriate spiritual goal for Colorado's hyper-fitness culture), as well as the aforementioned commitment to fellowship. The senior pastor now plans to connect study curriculum for small groups with the topics covered at weekend services.

The second Energized Church is located in Hopkinton, Massachusetts, a town that's best known as the starting point for the Boston Marathon. So perhaps it's not coincidental that this church chose to define discipleship as a clear set of stepping-stones known as its Faith Path, which guides participants through five classes, each of which focuses on a core spiritual theme and a set of practices. An introductory class describes the vision and values that shape the church's identity, ideally motivating people to attend worship services. Then Faith 101 follows with a focus on salvation by grace, and the expectation that students will finish the class ready and eager to make a commitment to Christ, sign up for baptism, and join a small group. Faith 201 explores what it means to develop a personal relationship with God through spiritual practices and the discovery of spiritual gifts. Faith 301 encourages participation in the body of Christ through church membership; then Faith 401 matches attenders with accountability partners who will provide support for ongoing spiritual growth and discipline.

Interestingly, that second attribute—"discipline"—is derived from the same root word as *disciple*. Both relate to the act of behaving in accordance with a set of known rules and doctrine. More than any other archetype, the Energized Church demonstrates the spiritual link between these words with its focus on activating discipleship through clear language and frameworks that clarify how people should grow into disciples of Christ. Not surprisingly, Energized Churches often embrace a modified version of the Purpose Driven baseball diamond (like the Faith Path in the Massachusetts church), and it's not uncommon to find that they are fans of "Simple Church"—which speaks to their zeal for focused direction.

The downside to this impressive archetype may be found in the classic response from Energized Church leaders who are asked, "How do you define discipleship?" Typically there's hardly a pause before a pastor launches into a description of a seven-step strategy or a spiritual formation framework that's built into small groups or a set of classes required for membership. These pastors have cornered the market, so to speak, on the *what* of discipleship—in other words, they provide clear direction about *what* congregants need to do to become a follower of Jesus Christ. But sometimes in their enthusiasm for the *what*, pastors may lose or minimize the message about the *why*.

The risk for Energized Church congregants is that their great love and respect for their church may overshadow and, to some extent, impede their spiritual progress. In other words, their journey may unintentionally become more of a quest to deepen their bond with their church rather than a journey to develop an increasingly meaningful relationship with Christ.

When Willow Creek Community Church took stock of its findings from the original REVEAL survey in 2004, senior pastor Bill Hybels recognized the need for several strategic adjustments. Among them was the need for a change in language. The findings suggested that Willow had implied to its congregants that the central source for spiritual nourishment, education, and development would always be the church. So Willow clarified its position—and nowadays often reinforces it to congregants in a three-part message: "You're on a journey to develop a relationship with Christ. It's *your* journey. And the church's role in that journey is to be there to help you."

The purpose of this strategic shift was to keep people focused on the true target of Willow's discipleship efforts—which was *not* to immerse them more deeply in church activities. It was to encourage them to pursue a relationship of increasing devotion and significance

TROUBLED

COMPLACENT

EXTROVERTED

AVERAGE

INTROVERTED

SELF-MOTIVATED

ENERGIZED

VIBRANT

with Christ—one that can and should become relatively *independent* of support from the church.

"You're on a journey. It's *your* journey. We're here to help." It's a healthy reminder for the Energized Church to make sure the *why* of discipleship is always as clear as the *what*.

SIX FACTORS THAT SET THE ENERGIZED CHURCH APART

1. Happy Church

Congregants in Energized Churches think their church is doing an excellent job in helping them grow spiritually. They report very high satisfaction with the way their church is implementing all five Best Practice Principles (see Chart 8.1). In particular, they hold their leaders in high regard, with a satisfaction rating for the Heart of the Leadership Team second only to Vibrant Churches.

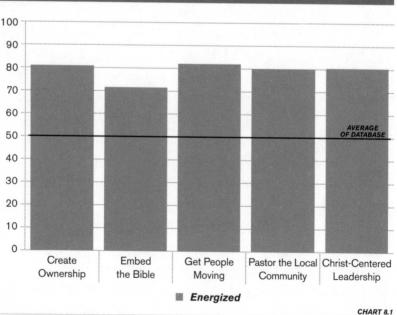

ENERGIZED CHURCHGOERS ARE HIGHLY SATISFIED WITH THEIR CHURCH

AVERAGE OF DATABASE

Create Ownership · Embed the Bible · Get People Moving · Pastor the Local Community · Christ-Centered Leadership

■ *Energized*

CHART 8.1

2. Perplexing Spirituality

The Energized Church's satisfaction profile looks like that of a thriving, highly effective church. As a result, we would expect to see similarly stellar results when we look at the congregation's level of engagement in personal spiritual practices and faith in action, as well as their adherence to the core beliefs. As shown in Chart 8.2, however, this isn't the case. Faith in action and personal spiritual practices are very average, and beliefs are only slightly above average. Energized churchgoers clearly notice and appreciate the investment their church makes in their spiritual growth, but they do not seem to be matching this investment by spending time outside of church on activities that would catalyze their progress. This pattern might make sense if Energized Churches had a high percentage of congregants in the Exploring and Growing in Christ stages of growth. But in reality, Energized Churches are slightly *below* average in the percentage of their congregants in these two stages. In short, it appears that Energized Church believers are not doing as much as we would expect to develop their faith on their own.

Why this perplexing spiritual pattern? As noted earlier, Energized Church congregants often gravitate toward defining their faith journey by their engagement with their church—meaning they may perceive that the time and energy devoted to church is generally sufficient for deepening their relationship with Christ. It's also possible that congregants haven't quite caught up with the discipleship vision and opportunities the church makes available to them. The good news is that the high satisfaction that characterizes the Energized Church gives its leaders a great "platform of permission" to inspire congregants to lead more fruitful and fulfilling spiritual lives.

3. Beloved Leaders Leading Well

Energized Church congregations love their senior pastor, reporting the highest level of satisfaction of any archetype. And leaders

TROUBLED
COMPLACENT
EXTROVERTED
AVERAGE
INTROVERTED
SELF-MOTIVATED
ENERGIZED
VIBRANT

FAITH IN ACTION AND SPIRITUAL PRACTICES ARE AVERAGE IN ENERGIZED CHURCHES

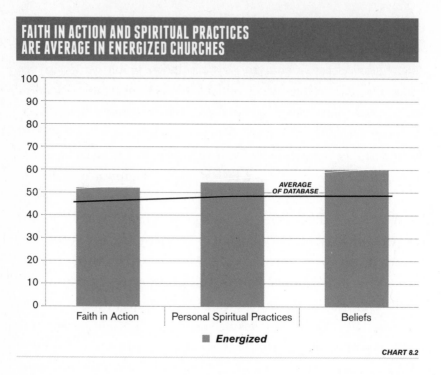

AVERAGE OF DATABASE

Faith in Action   Personal Spiritual Practices   Beliefs

■ *Energized*

CHART 8.2

of Energized Churches are more likely than others to describe their church as "visionary." These leaders focus on the right things, as reflected in the fact that they are more likely than other leaders to very strongly agree with two statements: "We challenge congregants to grow and take next steps," and "Our church leaders model and consistently reinforce how to grow spiritually." REVEAL research has shown that senior pastors who, like Energized Church leaders, prioritize modeling spiritual growth and challenging congregants to grow have a powerful effect on their congregants' spiritual journeys.[1] And Energized churchgoers express especially high levels of satisfaction with the way their church leaders provide them with these key spiritual catalysts.

[1] Greg L. Hawkins and Cally Parkinson, *Focus: The Top Ten Things People Want and Need from You and Your Church* (South Barrington, IL: Willow Creek Association, 2009).

4. Big on Small Groups

Leaders of Energized Churches prioritize small groups and recovery groups, considering them to be two of their church's "signature programs." Nearly 70 percent categorize small groups as one of their key distinctives, a rate that is higher than any other archetype. Their congregants also have the highest rate of participation in small groups, with an average of 55 percent of them attending a group at least twice each month.

5. Large Churches Growing Larger

Energized Churches tend to be very large, with an average weekend worship attendance of nearly one thousand adults. Moreover, 72 percent report that their attendance has grown over the past year. Few report declining attendance. Leaders of Energized Churches seem to focus a great deal of energy on their weekend services. And they very strongly agree (at twice the rate of leaders of other church archetypes) with the statement, "We provide a powerful and compelling corporate worship experience." Congregant satisfaction with the church's worship experience also is above average compared to other archetypes.

6. Young Churches with Young Congregants

One in five Energized Churches is a recent church plant, founded since 2000. In all, 36 percent began in 1990 or later. As a result, very few congregants in Energized Churches have attended their church for ten years or more. Also, few of their congregants are over the age of fifty. On both of these metrics, Energized Churches are distinct from all other archetypes. They are more likely than other church types to be located in the Middle Atlantic (New York, New Jersey, and Pennsylvania) and East South Central (Alabama, Kentucky, Mississippi, and Tennessee) regions of the United States. Energized Churches are, however, no different from other church types in their congregations' levels of education, income, or ethnic/racial diversity.

TROUBLED
COMPLACENT
EXTROVERTED
AVERAGE
INTROVERTED
SELF-MOTIVATED
ENERGIZED
VIBRANT

The case study that follows provides a classic Energized Church profile, led by a pastor who made very focused, strategic decisions to take their already dynamic spiritual culture to another level of devotion to Jesus.

....

AN ENERGIZED-TO-VIBRANT CASE STUDY: NEW LIFE ASSEMBLY, KEARNEY, NEBRASKA

Lead Pastor Bob Wine was clearly ahead of the curve.

In 2004, as research professionals grappled for months with the results of Willow Creek's original congregational survey and its implications in the area of spiritual growth, Bob—who was in the midst of his more than thirty years of serving New Life Assembly in Kearney, Nebraska—was also focused on spiritual growth. He was purposefully in pursuit of the most effective ways to help his congregants move toward spiritual maturity. Convinced that spiritual growth is the church's primary objective, Bob had even taught on four stages along that pathway to maturity—stages he described as The Babe, The Little Child, The Young Man, and The Father. (All with similarities, it turns out, to REVEAL's Exploring Christ, Growing in Christ, Close to Christ, and Christ-Centered categories.)

When Bob learned about REVEAL, he was eager for his congregation to participate. "It was right down the alley of what questions we needed answered," Bob remembers. "It was just a great fit for us."

✦ ✦ ✦

Begun in July 1954, in a tent pitched on a vacant lot in Kearney, New Life has undergone many significant changes during six decades of serving its semirural community in Nebraska's midsection. When Bob arrived there in 1979, Sunday service attendance was just over a hundred people; today it is close to seven hundred. And when asked to describe those attenders, he explains, "We are Assembly of God, but we don't have a whole lot of Assembly people. Those who come to our church are basically people who really want more of God. Who want to know the truth. Who want to be discipled."

To satisfy those desires, Bob has long championed the importance of spiritual growth. Describing his leadership style as "more strategic than charismatic," he explains that his church already had many spiritual growth initiatives in place when the congregation took its first REVEAL survey in October 2008. Those initiatives, which continue today, clearly were a contributing factor in New Life's strong initial survey results—results that included a Spiritual Vitality Index (SVI) of 78, with 32 percent of the congregation falling in the most mature Christ-Centered segment and 38 percent of congregants paired with a spiritual mentor.

With the firm foundation reflected in these impressive results, Bob and his leaders made two important—but seemingly simple—decisions.

Leadership Decision #1 was to stick with what's working.

Although New Life would use its initial survey results in innovative ways, its first order of business was to affirm its spiritual growth philosophy and its commitment to two related strategies.

(1) *Spiritual Growth Philosophy: Spirit, Soul, and Body*

"This is one of the things that has been part of who I am for a very long time," Bob says when talking about the concept of spirit, soul, and body. "And anybody who comes to the church in a year's time is going to hear it more than once. I use it as a tool to explain how we need to focus on our spirit—and what we need to do to follow God." Bob teaches that the spirit, often described as conscience or intuition, best helps people sense God's presence. He uses illustrations from the Bible as well as his own personal experience to teach this concept—a key component, he believes, of the spiritual growth his congregation has achieved. "We've placed a great deal of value on not letting our

TROUBLED

COMPLACENT

EXTROVERTED

AVERAGE

INTROVERTED

SELF-MOTIVATED

ENERGIZED

VIBRANT

mind and emotions govern us," he explains, "but rather on letting that intuitive side [the spirit] govern our life—and then letting our mind and emotion carry out what we are sensing."

(2) *Video-Driven Strategy for Small Groups*

Small groups, which Bob describes as New Life's "most significant discipling tool," have a purpose far beyond social interaction. "They do have a social component, but that's not what they're about," Bob says. "They are designed to help people get into the Word; to pray together; to help them grow in their spiritual faith journey." Toward that end, the church offers direction and resources. Each fall, for instance, small groups are typically asked to align their teaching with the new series of sermons. Most of the time, though, groups are free to choose their own topics—topics supported by a large video library collection, in which all resources are classified by the spiritual growth components they best reinforce. (Should the group opt to focus on prayer, for instance, it might check out Jim Cymbala's *When God's People Pray*.) These resources have the added benefit, Bob explains, of not requiring small group leaders to also take on teaching duties.

(3) *Mentoring Strategy*

An ongoing relationship with a compatible spiritual mentor is one of the most effective—but often one of the hardest to attain—of all spiritual practices. How do we identify the right person? Explain what we're looking for? Make the ask? At New Life Assembly, congregants desiring such one-on-one discipleship know exactly what to do—simply contact a designated volunteer whom Bob Wine describes as "very, very, very good at discipling." This individual not only coaches and coordinates the church's network of mentors, he also acts as a matchmaker of sorts. "We'll put it in the bulletin every once in a while, or do a sermon on it," Bob says. "And we'll say, 'If you're interested, just contact the office.'" Then mentors and those looking to be mentored are paired up and supported on an ongoing basis.

Leadership Decision #2 was to delegate the creation of next steps to its congregation.

When churches receive their initial REVEAL results, either the senior pastor alone or the larger leadership team reviews and digests the results. Then, typically, after sharing selected aspects of the survey report with the congregation, leaders launch initiatives designed to address the church's areas of greatest need. New Life Assembly began with the usual first step. Then it departed from the norm, turning the results over to several cross-sectional groups of congregants and requesting their input. Each group studied a different aspect of the REVEAL report, discussed what those results indicated, and put together a presentation on what they had discovered and how they thought the church might respond.

"That obviously created a great deal of ownership," Bob explains. It also set the stage for several deliberate, concrete steps forward— initiatives chosen for their strong potential to foster spiritual growth.

New Life Got People Moving—by Communicating a Clear Discipleship Path

The church's first step forward involved the creation of a tract, an attractively designed and illustrated six-panel handout that describes REVEAL's four segments of spiritual maturity, the three transitions from one segment to the next, the top catalysts for each of those transitions, a prayer, a description of crossing the line of faith in Christ, and contact information for the church—all of which is easily readable and, when folded, measures a mere two-by-three inches. (You almost need to see it to believe it!)

"We gave everybody one—and also had it on our screens so we could explain it and everyone could follow along," Bob says. "We distributed them that way a number of times, and some people have also taken large quantities of them to share with their families and friends. It's hands-on, and a way to help people move forward. Rather

TROUBLED

COMPLACENT

EXTROVERTED

AVERAGE

INTROVERTED

SELF-MOTIVATED

ENERGIZED

VIBRANT

than condemning anyone, it's a great way to ask, 'Where are you on this journey? And do you want to move forward?'"

In early 2009, Bob offered a sermon on the handout, so people could assess where they were personally. Then he launched a series on each stage of maturity and the transitions between those stages. He also spent one Sunday focusing on the "stalled" category of congregants, offering ways these individuals might move forward.

New Life Embedded the Bible—with "Fuel for the Journey"

Then, in the fall of 2009, after the REVEAL report had been widely shared and discussed, Bob taught a series on spiritual disciplines. The church's small groups all reinforced this teaching, and each individual in the church once again left with a supportive creative resource: a two-and-a-half-inch square plastic box filled with forty-five bright yellow cards entitled FUEL for the JOURNEY / Energy Pack.

This resource, which had been initiated by the congregational study groups described above, was then developed by Bob and his pastoral staff. Introductory cards defined spiritual disciplines, provided a list of them, introduced the process, and offered a prayer. Then the next forty cards—one for each day of the congregation's journey—named and defined a single spiritual discipline, provided specific directions related to that discipline, and added a relevant quote. The first card, on PRAYER, reads: "Private and corporate, yet intimate, heartfelt communication with God at a deeper level than your norm." And "Pray that God will guide and strengthen you during this spiritual discipline adventure." At the bottom is a quote from Corrie ten Boom: "Don't pray when you feel like it. Have an appointment with the Lord and keep it. A man is powerful on his knees." (Other PRAYER cards, featuring additional information, are located further along in the pack.)

Bob's sermons referred to the cards, typically combining disciplines and describing them in practical terms. "People really enjoyed it," he says, "and many of them continued to use the cards long after the series ended." Bob says New Life has come back to this topic—and this resource—at various times in the years since. "We have been keeping it in front of people," he says, "but not driving it so much that it becomes a nuisance to them."

In September 2010, a sermon series on spiritual gifts built on the church's ongoing emphasis on hearing God's voice. They focused on what Scripture has to say on the subject and how to practice those gifts in very practical terms. "Again, if it's a spiritual gift, then you are going to have to follow your spirit, rather than your head or emotions," Bob says. "So we key in on that. And of course this is all very relevant to the spiritual growth discussions in REVEAL."

And speaking of REVEAL, what did New Life Assembly's follow-up survey, taken in October 2010, have to say? That the church's SVI went up ten points, to 88—putting them in the top 5 percent of all REVEAL churches. That personal spiritual practices—including Bible reading, reflection on Scripture, prayer to seek guidance, and solitude—all went up in statistically meaningful ways. That the Close to Christ segment increased from 26 to 30 percent of the congregation (the Christ-Centered segment remained high, at 31 percent). Also, that the already high numbers for satisfaction with the church (64 percent) and pastor (83 percent) zoomed ahead to 76 and 90 percent, respectively.

+ + +

Clearly, New Life Assembly will not rest on its laurels, but continue to focus on movement toward spiritual maturity. In addition, Bob will continue to encourage his fellow pastors to do the same. "I'm a real advocate of REVEAL. It provides a map. It can help people see where they are and know what to do to move forward. The driving force [for pastors] must be to follow Jesus' greatest command and shepherd their people's hearts and not just their minds or behavior. REVEAL helps with that, and if more of my colleagues would step up to it, I think it would be a win for the body of Christ."

THE HOPE FOR THE ENERGIZED CHURCH

There's a point in every athlete's career when the need arises for a coach to help reach the next level of performance. In team sports, coaching is a natural expectation—it's part of the formula that leads to athletic development and success. But in individual sports— like swimming, ice-skating, and running—coaching is more often reserved for the elite. Most people pursue these sports for fun or exercise rather than to hone their skills for organized competition.

Spiritual growth shares characteristics of both types of sports. Like a team sport, where a coach urges a group to achieve a certain level of performance, spiritual growth benefits from encouragement and equipping provided by the church and from participating with the church body in regular group experiences like Sunday services, small groups, and serving initiatives. With this level of "coaching," people can advance to very mature levels of faith.

However, it is possible that spiritual advancement can fall short— particularly at higher levels of maturity where church support tends to weaken. Should people at that point be proficient at "self-feeding"? Should they be able to proceed sufficiently with their spiritual development, working for the most part under their own steam with the help of the Holy Spirit? Probably. But it's also possible that a spiritual growth "gap" exists that might be filled very effectively by an individual coach—much like the individual coaches who step in to guide and counsel elite athletes. This type of individual coach—known as a spiritual mentor—is the hope for the Energized Church.

Many of the strongest churches in the REVEAL database consider spiritual mentoring a high priority. Some, like Bob Wine's New Life church, have the good fortune to find a trusted discipleship enthusiast either on staff or in their congregation who will shepherd the mentoring process, recruiting mentor candidates and matching them with people who want to be mentored. Most of the churches, however, craft intentional mentoring strategies that include some or all of the following factors:

- They choose or create a *standard mentoring curriculum* so that mentors do not have to invent their own spiritual growth syllabus. One such program is the Navigators 2:7 Series, which also provides instruction for mentors in a book called *The Ways of the Alongsider*. Another noteworthy mentoring resource is Radical Mentoring by Regi Campbell, a twelve-month program incorporating topics like character, grace, and spiritual warfare that is specifically targeted to men. The companion program for women is Titus 2.
- They pursue a *"soft launch,"* meaning the mentoring strategy is treated as an organic process rather than a ministry program. Specifically, the curriculum is introduced first to the church staff—with either the senior pastor serving as the mentor for key staff members or staff members mentoring a select group of lay leaders.
- Typically, *mentoring expands informally* as people become aware that this opportunity is available, although some churches use the Alpha program as a channel to connect new believers with mentors.

In whatever form it takes, mentoring has great potential to elevate spiritual development in the Energized Church. It takes advantage of the high level of trust and satisfaction that the church already enjoys—since congregants would automatically consider a church-sponsored mentoring process in a favorable light. It also benefits from the relational connections already in place in its small group system, which is typically a strong and popular channel for fellowship in an Energized Church. Mentor candidates could emerge naturally from this kind of healthy interpersonal ministry.

TROUBLED

COMPLACENT

EXTROVERTED

AVERAGE

INTROVERTED

SELF-MOTIVATED

ENERGIZED

VIBRANT

> ## Symptoms of an Energized Church
>
> A church likely falls into the Energized Church archetype if these three primary characteristics exist:
>
> 1. *Satisfaction runs high, and people are particularly happy with the senior pastor.* Pastors sense nothing but great enthusiasm for church vision and initiatives. Church leaders receive praise and accolades much more often than critiques regarding decisions and the strategic direction of the church. They are admired and respected, and this is particularly true of the senior pastor.
> 2. *An energized "buzz" infuses the culture of the church.* Small groups are thriving. Church attendance is growing. Weekend services rock. Church activities seem imbued with an energy that unifies congregants and pours out through expressions of worship and service.
> 3. *Spirituality may be more church-centered than Christ-centered.* Pastors would be unsurprised to find that congregants do not make much of a distinction between their devotion to the church and their devotion to Jesus. While they are well aware that they're on a spiritual journey, Energized Church congregants—especially the more mature believers—seem to lean more heavily than they should into the church to actively guide and equip them for that mission.

Mentoring may fill a "gap" that exists not only in the Energized Church, but in other archetypes as well. Evidence from REVEAL suggests that many of the most mature followers of Christ are under-challenged—and every church congregation includes some percentage of those Christ-Centered followers. They are not unmotivated. They just seem a little lost, or perhaps unaware of the powerful possibilities that exist for living out their faith in much more dramatic and productive ways.

All elite athletes need a coach—someone who can help them see their blind spots, suggest new techniques to enhance performance, and provide comfort when obstacles or defeat threaten their confidence. Followers of Jesus deserve no less. Thankfully, they already have the best coach possible! But sometimes the whispers of the Holy Spirit are hard to hear—and it would be nice to have someone to help us turn up the volume.

NEW LIFE ASSEMBLY CHURCH: 2014 UPDATE

What's the single biggest difference in New Life since the case study?

New Life Assembly Church has a new lead pastor. In 2013, Bob Wine became the superintendent of Assembly of God churches for the state of Nebraska. His successor, Jeff Baker, brings with him nine years of ministry experience at New Life as well as six years of church planting in Omaha's inner-city neighborhoods. Jeff says he's an "outreach-driven guy" with a passion to leverage video technology to create "life-giving churches" in rural environments.

What's new in New Life's discipleship strategies and culture since the case study?

To enlist the energy and enthusiasm of New Life's congregation for his vision of planting healthy rural churches, Jeff planted a church—called the Gym Venue—within New Life's large facility. The teaching is identical to the traditional service, but the more casual ambiance attracts a different crowd. Jeff felt it was critical to his vision of rural outreach to prove to New Life's veteran attenders that another church model—one that could be reproduced in rural settings—could coexist with New Life and also be financially sustainable.

What's next on the horizon for New Life?

New Life has two significant initiatives at hand. The first is the rollout in September 2014 of their first rural church plant in North Platte, a community ninety miles away. The second is the rollout of a discipleship pathway that builds on their original framework using the REVEAL segments. This pathway is action-oriented, using icons and verbs to communicate spiritual movement. For example, Exploring Christ will become "Step Over the Line"; Growing in Christ, "Walk Steady"; Close to Christ, "Run Straight"; and Christ-Centered, "Give It ALL." Jeff's vision is that soon all church activities will be associated with icons indicating their most appropriate spiritual maturity level.

AN ENERGIZED DESTINATION

In the case studies presented to this point, most of the churches have, over time, shifted from their original archetype to the Energized archetype. The key to understanding why this pattern is so common is to consider how change typically occurs in churches that want to move from struggling or treading water to thriving. Church leaders receive their REVEAL results, register their disappointment with how their church is doing, and decide to implement some strategies that they hope will result in a revival of spiritual growth in their congregation. Congregants begin to notice that their church is doing something new and different. Spurred by these initiatives, they may experience some growth in their beliefs and begin to engage in spiritual practices and faith-in-action activities more frequently.

Then, a year or so later, they take the survey again. What has changed? Usually, satisfaction with their church's role in their spiritual growth has risen considerably. Changes in congregant beliefs and behaviors typically take more time to register and are smaller in magnitude than changes in satisfaction. If a Complacent Church moves from low to average levels of spiritual maturity and maintains or increases their satisfaction with the church, it becomes an Energized Church. If an Introverted Church's satisfaction increases and they maintain their above-average beliefs and spiritual practices, it also becomes an Energized Church. Extroverted Churches that raise their beliefs and spiritual practices to average levels will be typed as Energized as well. In this case, the Energized archetype represents a church in transition, where leaders are taking important steps to create a more spiritually vibrant environment for their congregation's growth, and the congregation responds as they experience the catalyzing effects of these changes.

TROUBLED

COMPLACENT

EXTROVERTED

AVERAGE

INTROVERTED

SELF-MOTIVATED

ENERGIZED

VIBRANT

CHAPTER 9
THE VIBRANT CHURCH

"The Spirit gives life; the flesh counts for nothing" (John 6:63).

Although no pastors have quoted these words from Jesus in conversations after taking the REVEAL survey, their very direct questions often align with the point he was making. That's because pastors can see the research as producing a "to do" list for church leaders, one that seemingly ignores the role of the Holy Spirit. "Where is God in all of this?" they sometimes ask. "Doesn't the impact of the church rest on his power through the Holy Spirit?" Their underlying question is essentially this: What are the relative roles of the church and the Holy Spirit as they partner to help people grow into disciples of Christ?

The Vibrant Church provides the answer to that question—because this church archetype is full of the life that the "Spirit gives."

In fact, the meaning of the word *vibrant*—full of life—perfectly captures the dynamic, spiritually effervescent nature of these churches. To open one of their reports is to experience something akin to a breathtaking spiritual fireworks display as it explodes with facts testifying to a deep devotion to Christ, a profound love for all people, great appreciation for their church, and—yes—the life-giving power of the Holy Spirit.

But the distinction of the Vibrant Church compared to other archetypes is *not* that it somehow benefits from a higher-octane dose of the Holy Spirit. The secret to its clearly exceptional spiritual fruit is that the Vibrant Church does a better job than any other archetype of *opening the doors*—of breaking through to people's hearts, minds, and souls—so that the life the Spirit wants to give is unmistakable and embraced.

How this *opening the doors* is accomplished is summarized in chapter 1's description of the five best practices churches can use to advance spiritual growth (see Chart 1.6). Born out of earlier REVEAL research, these practices were instrumental to the discovery of the church archetypes. But while they have been very useful in terms of research and analysis, they may be too abstract—or too daunting—to be of practical help to the pastors, who almost always ask at the end of their REVEAL results consultation: "What's my next step?"

Chapter 10 is devoted to describing such "next steps"—customized by archetype—that will best enable spiritual traction to occur. But becoming "vibrant" is a high bar, so in recognition of the somewhat overwhelming nature of that goal, we offer the following story of how one church that was far from vibrant in 2008 became one of the most "full of life" churches in the REVEAL database.

You may remember Mark Ashton from chapter 6, the pastor from Omaha whose first reaction to his REVEAL results was to hide them from his elders. Two years into his first senior pastor position, his church's initial report—which revealed an Introverted Church with a below-average SVI of 63—was discouraging. But Mark resolved to *open doors* so the Spirit could breathe life into his congregation. He did so . . .

- by launching "whole church spiritual adventures," first guiding the congregation through an eight-week study that integrated weekend services and small group curriculum on the life of Elijah (1 and 2 Kings). A twelve-week study on David followed, then five weeks on the book of Acts. Finally, in 2012, Mark devoted one full year to walking *everyone*—from adults to children—through a chronological study of the entire Bible;

- by defining what becoming a disciple of Christ looks like in concrete terms, using the acronym RISKS (**R**elies on God—**I**nitiates Interest in the Bible—**S**erves Others—**K**ingdom Investor—**S**hape into Christlikeness) in order to clarify expectations for newcomers and members alike regarding their spiritual destination and next steps; and

- by targeting real neighborhood transformation in one of the most impoverished areas of Omaha, becoming the invisible partner of a struggling local church—not only providing financial resources, but also sending hundreds of volunteers to serve in multiple venues—all wearing T-shirts promoting the partner church, which has now tripled in size.

Christ Community Church's attendance has grown as well, from 2,500 to 3,500 in the last four years, as it moved from being a lackluster, unhappy Introverted Church into a Vibrant Church that—based on its REVEAL results—is firing on all spiritual cylinders.

This story is important for two reasons: First, it reinforces the REVEAL conclusion that all churches have the potential to become "vibrant." And even more importantly, it illustrates in practical terms the church's role in that process. Do the words of Jesus—"the Spirit gives life"—mean that the church is to wait passively in anticipation of the Spirit's arrival? What seems more likely is that the role of the church is much like that of a mother in labor, actively working to give birth to the precious life emerging from her womb.

The church's role is not to "give life." Only the Spirit does that. Rather, the unique and very important role of the church is to *open*

TROUBLED

COMPLACENT

EXTROVERTED

AVERAGE

INTROVERTED

SELF-MOTIVATED

ENERGIZED

VIBRANT

the doors so that the life the Spirit wants to give has the best possible chance to thrive.

SIX FACTORS THAT SET THE VIBRANT CHURCH APART

1. Fully Surrendered Disciples

In Vibrant Churches, more than 60 percent of the congregation is in the Close to Christ and Christ-Centered stages of spiritual growth. Vibrant Churches soar to the top of the distribution of churches when it comes to their core beliefs, engagement in personal spiritual practices, and putting their faith into action (see Chart 9.1). Nearly 40 percent of these congregants very strongly agree that they are willing to risk everything in their lives for the sake of Jesus Christ—a statistic that is fourteen percentage points higher than the database average and five points higher than Self-Motivated Churches (the

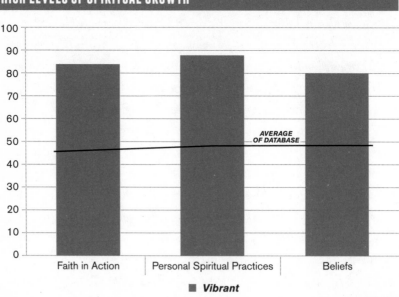

IN VIBRANT CHURCHES, CONGREGANTS EXHIBIT HIGH LEVELS OF SPIRITUAL GROWTH

AVERAGE OF DATABASE

Faith in Action — Personal Spiritual Practices — Beliefs

■ *Vibrant*

CHART 9.1

only other archetype that comes close). The spiritually thriving nature of Vibrant Churches is also reflected in their average SVI of 88, which is eighteen points above average and higher than the average for any other church type by at least nine points.

2. Extremely Satisfied

More than one-fourth of Vibrant Church congregants are extremely satisfied with the way their church is helping them grow spiritually—a percentage ten points above the average of the REVEAL database and higher than any other archetype. Not only do Vibrant Church congregants give their church high marks for all five Best Practice Principles (see Chart 9.2), they give their leadership high marks as well—with 56 percent saying they are extremely satisfied with their senior pastor, a statistic 30 percent higher than the average for all churches.

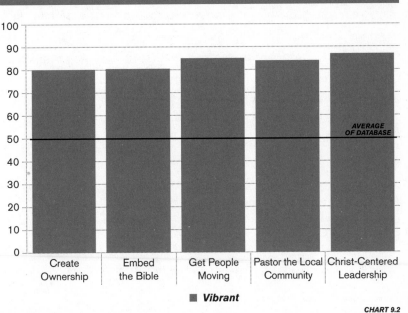

SATISFACTION IS VERY HIGH IN A VIBRANT CHURCH

AVERAGE OF DATABASE

Create Ownership / Embed the Bible / Get People Moving / Pastor the Local Community / Christ-Centered Leadership

■ *Vibrant*

CHART 9.2

TROUBLED

COMPLACENT

EXTROVERTED

AVERAGE

INTROVERTED

SELF-MOTIVATED

ENERGIZED

VIBRANT

3. Large and Growing Congregations

Collectively, the Vibrant Churches in REVEAL's database have an average attendance of more than 1,100 adults—higher than any other archetype. Churches of this size are rare, comprising less than 2 percent of all Protestant churches in the United States.[1] However, it doesn't take a thousand worship attenders to become a Vibrant Church. About 25 percent of Vibrant Churches have a weekend worship attendance of fewer than 250 adults. Vibrant Churches of all sizes tend to be growing in size as their members share their faith with those outside the church and newcomers are attracted to their thriving spiritual vibe.

4. Equipped and on the Move

Compared to the other archetypes, Vibrant Church congregations have the lowest percentage that reports their spiritual growth is stalled—and the highest percentage that reports they are growing at a rapid pace. These statistics are not surprising, considering what Vibrant Church leaders say are their church's distinctive ministry offerings. Twice as many of them name having a structured spiritual development path as one of their top five programs. In addition to doing all they can to keep their congregation moving, Vibrant Churches equip their people to put their faith in action. The percentage of Vibrant Church congregants who say they know and use their spiritual gifts and feel equipped to share their faith is 50 percent higher than the average for all churches. More than half of their congregations serve those in need once a month or more, and nearly a third report having spiritual conversations with nonbelievers on a regular basis.

5. Focused Leaders

Previous REVEAL research shows that congregants need to be spiritually challenged by their senior pastor in order to grow.[2] As noted

---

[1] National Congregations Study, 2012.
[2] Greg L. Hawkins and Cally Parkinson, *Focus: The Top Ten Things People Want and Need from You and Your Church*, (South Barrington, IL: Willow Creek Association, 2009).

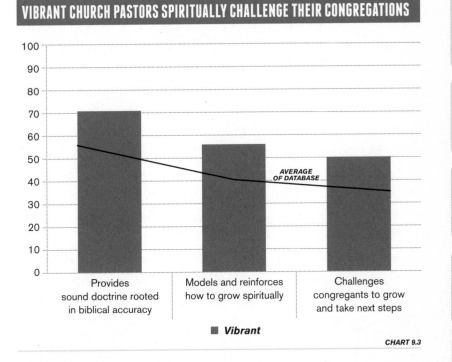

VIBRANT CHURCH PASTORS SPIRITUALLY CHALLENGE THEIR CONGREGATIONS

AVERAGE OF DATABASE

Provides sound doctrine rooted in biblical accuracy

Models and reinforces how to grow spiritually

Challenges congregants to grow and take next steps

■ *Vibrant*

CHART 9.3

earlier, congregants in Vibrant Churches are very satisfied with their senior pastors. But it's worth noting here that in the eyes of their congregants, these pastors excel in particular at three specific aspects of delivering spiritual challenge, which are described in Chart 9.3. As shown in this graphic, their congregations' satisfaction with the level of spiritual challenge delivered by their senior pastor is well above average, and the highest of all church archetypes. Leaders of Vibrant Churches are also much more likely than leaders of other archetypes to very strongly agree that they prioritize these aspects of spiritual challenge as they lead their church.

6. Diverse, Southern Demographics

While Vibrant Churches are more likely than other types to be located in the South and in urban settings, the majority of them

TROUBLED

COMPLACENT

EXTROVERTED

AVERAGE

INTROVERTED

SELF-MOTIVATED

ENERGIZED

VIBRANT

reside in suburban locales. Most of their congregants have not completed college and have family incomes below seventy-five thousand dollars. Vibrant Churches stand out from other types in their degree of racial/ethnic diversity, with more than 75 percent of them enjoying a mix of congregants from various backgrounds.

The following case study describes a Vibrant Church that became *more* vibrant, based on its second REVEAL survey. This church exhibits most of the archetype's classic characteristics, except for a few demographics. It is located on the West Coast, not in the South, and its diversity mix is in the single (3 to 4 percent) versus double digits. Its weekend attendance, while still growing at 800, is below the 1,100 Vibrant Church average. The most critical factors of this archetype, however, are right on track, underscoring the observation noted earlier—that becoming a Vibrant Church is an opportunity available to all churches.

A VIBRANT CHURCH CASE STUDY:
FAMILY CHURCH, SUTHERLIN, OREGON

"It was like pouring gasoline on a fire."

Lead pastor Ed Wilgus's analogy is a perfect fit, because when the Family Church received its initial REVEAL survey results, their fire was already burning. Their report from that March 2009 study included impressive results in several categories, summarized by a well-above-average Spiritual Vitality Index (SVI) of 84.

So how did Ed, teaching pastor Paul Glazner, and their leadership team respond? With confidence, making two key decisions right off the bat that guided their church to even more extraordinary spiritual gains that would be reflected in their second survey two years later.

Leadership Decision #1 was to dismiss all doubts that their spiritual growth plan was on target.

The REVEAL results enabled Ed and his team to set aside any inclinations to second-guess the church's spiritual and strategic direction. "I can't tell you how clarifying and how exciting it was to no longer be thinking, 'Well, is *this* the right direction?'" recalls Ed. "We just said, 'This is it!' and went forward, with no more discussion of what we might do instead."

Leadership Decision #2 was a natural by-product of #1: *Aim everything* at accelerating the plan.

Understanding the powerful strategy Family Church uses to inspire its congregants to pursue spiritual growth is crucial to understanding why and how this Vibrant Church became even stronger in the aftermath of its first REVEAL survey. But before describing what they do, a review of church history will provide a context for why what they do is so effective.

The church, located in southwestern Oregon, about an hour south of Eugene and the same distance east of the Pacific Ocean, grew out of a Bible study in 1974. Paul Glazner came in 1986 to lead the church, which at that point had thirty-five congregants. In 2006, after some twenty years as its pastor, Paul felt the church of four-hundred-plus attenders had hit something of a plateau. Ed Wilgus, a staff pastor, was invited to take on the role of lead pastor. Paul would continue as teaching pastor, and the two men would share leadership of the church's staff and congregation.

The resulting structure flies in the face of conventional wisdom, which suggests that pastors in senior roles should exit when new ones come on board. But Paul and Ed's arrangement has worked very well, and today the church's three-service weekends welcome some eight hundred people, most of whom reside in or around Sutherlin, a community of seven thousand. Crucial to their progress has been the

TROUBLED

COMPLACENT

EXTROVERTED

AVERAGE

INTROVERTED

SELF-MOTIVATED

ENERGIZED

VIBRANT

two pastors' commitment to fostering a grace-filled, loving, accepting culture. "Whatever we do, we are trying to deepen this culture," Ed explains. "We are not nearly as much about adding programs as we are about developing this organic culture of encouragement and spiritual growth."

To put some muscle behind this shared vision of "organic culture," the pastors turned to a popular framework for church assimilation found in thousands of churches across the country, one that was already in place at Family Church.

In fact, Family Church had become a Purpose Driven Church in 1996, using the well-known baseball diamond illustration to describe the progression of steps toward congregant education and assimilation. According to Ed, "[The Purpose Driven model] has a discipleship side to it, but one of the challenges with a model like that is it's very programmatic."

Then came REVEAL. "Once we saw REVEAL, we began to see the power of incorporating that into our language and our process. The REVEAL continuum was more of a personal journey," says Ed, "so we added that to the diamond, and now that continuum drives what we do all around the bases."

The power behind the Family Church spiritual growth strategy is this merger—bringing together the Purpose Driven model, which helps congregants know "what" they should do to grow their relationship with Christ, with the insights from REVEAL, which help them understand the "why" behind the "what." And true to their innovative inclinations, Family Church's pastoral team decided to overlay those bases with their own language about the four stages of spiritual growth—reflecting the church's resolve to evangelize Seekers, educate Students, equip Servants, and empower Stewards. The following example of utilizing REVEAL Best Practice Principles sheds light on why this personalized pathway of spiritual growth seems to work so well.

Family Church Gets Their People Moving—by Pointing Seekers in the Right Direction

Seekers enjoy a significant part of Family Church's attention. They are made welcome and encouraged to attend services, where messages purposefully include some content directed toward the unconvinced. They are strongly encouraged to attend the Purpose Driven 101 Connecting class, where they are invited to join a small group and—most importantly—they are encouraged to pursue various church-related opportunities designed to help them answer the question "What is a Christ follower?" The church's vision and its four-stage discipleship pathway of Seekers, Students, Servants, and Stewards are introduced in this initial classroom experience.

Seekers are also encouraged to participate in First Serve opportunities to help people in need. Serving is, after all, a fundamental component of Family Church's culture—so much so that Ed says people have occasionally left the church because of its high expectations in this area. Individuals can serve one another and serve together through their small group, as part of a ministry team, and during a twice-yearly church-wide community service project. "We're not a church where you can attend and feel comfortable just coming week after week without getting involved somewhere," Ed explains. "We have created a culture where people understand that if you're going to be part of this community of believers, you need to be committed to each other . . . and we will help you find an appropriate place to serve."

Family Church Embeds the Bible—by Educating Students Through Classes and Mentoring

For those congregants who have recently confessed their faith in Christ—or who have yet to grow very far beyond an earlier acceptance—Family Church steps up to the role of educator. And like conscientious teachers everywhere, they have developed precise definitions of what their Students need to learn. This includes salvation by grace and the authority of the Bible, as well as acceptance of the Trinity, belief in a personal God, and the desire for Christ to come first in the believer's life.

A variety of core classes address various aspects of each Student's need to grow in Christ, to grow in his or her family, to grow in God's Word, and to grow in truth. These classes include a modified version of Purpose Driven 201, where congregants are encouraged to commit to personal spiritual practices ranging from reading the entire Bible to daily prayer and Scripture reading. Students very often achieve much of their progress through mentoring.

Like serving, mentoring is an integral part of the church's culture, rather than one choice among a menu of options a person can choose from. ("I couldn't even tell you how many of these relationships exist," says Ed.) Introduced after their first REVEAL survey and available to all attenders, mentoring relationships usually involve three or four people—known by their shorthand description of "triads" and "quads." These mentoring connections typically begin with relationships that already exist, such as small groups and ministry teams, and then go deeper. And while they are important to congregants in every stage of spiritual development, they are of particular value to those who are Students.

Family Church Creates Ownership—by Equipping Servants to Become Church Leaders

The church describes Servants as those who feel close to Christ and who depend on Him daily for guidance. Very often, that guidance moves these individuals toward serving in the church—as ministry volunteers, for example, or as mentors or small group leaders. And the church, in turn, is committed to equipping Servants for such responsibilities.

Family Church's small groups are likely on the verge of further expansion. But the growth they anticipate does not refer to mere numbers. It primarily refers to the increased discipleship that will likely result from the church's stepped-up emphasis on getting all small group members into their Bibles—a practice that coincides with a challenge to weekend service attenders to spend time in God's Word on a daily basis.

Of course, small group growth will depend in large part on the availability and support of Servants, and Ed acknowledges that people can be hesitant to make this commitment. "Each fall, we invite everybody into a small group," he says. "It's also a time when we really challenge people to step out and lead. We say, 'Try it for six weeks and see what it's like.'"

When a Servant steps forward, the church's commitment to equipping gears up—with a video curriculum for use in group gatherings, for instance, and leadership development opportunities that include courses like Lead Like Jesus and the 301 Serving class from the Purpose Driven Church model. Then there is the church's ever-present cultural goal of fostering discipleship, made stronger by its post-REVEAL commitment to focus on getting people deeper into the Word—a commitment that benefits all congregants as it further equips Servants.

Family Church Pastors the Community—by Empowering Stewards to Give Their Lives to God

Stewards, the most spiritually mature segment of Family Church's congregants, consider their relationship with Jesus as the most important relationship in their lives—the one that guides everything they do. "The endgame is what we call stewardship," Ed explains. "It's giving your life away. It's not 'God's here for me.' It's 'I'm here for God.'"

The empowerment of their Stewards directly benefits the church's ministry, enabling it to serve some eight hundred congregants with

TROUBLED

COMPLACENT

EXTROVERTED

AVERAGE

INTROVERTED

SELF-MOTIVATED

ENERGIZED

VIBRANT

less than a dozen full-time staff members. Stewards teach classes, organize projects, lead ministry teams, and coach teams of small group leaders. They advise; they counsel; they see themselves not so much as workers for God, but as people open and willing for God to do His work through them.

But the distinction of the Steward is more about the heart than their behavior. As noted earlier, Family Church's "organic culture" is marked by a strong commitment to service. Stewards are asked to take that commitment to its highest level—challenging them, according to Ed, to determine, "Where has God really called you? Are you serving in a place where you are gifted? Are you living by the power of God to serve—as opposed to the power of yourself?" Tough questions. And as is the case at every stage of their discipleship path, there's a class—similar to Purpose Driven 401—that helps people picture what their own version of the Christ-Centered "endgame" looks like, and what life changes that implies.

✦ ✦ ✦

In April 2011, Family Church congregants responded to a second REVEAL survey. Church satisfaction rose from an already strong 67 to an impressive 78 percent (the REVEAL norm is 52 percent). A remarkable 55 percent said they served those in need through the church (the norm is 25 percent) and a similar percentage reported serving those in need on their own. About 45 percent said they connect with mentors, 37 percent reflect on Scripture daily, and 41 percent agreed they would "risk everything that's important in my life" for the cause of Christ. All of these measures are at least 50 percent greater than the REVEAL average.

With a new SVI of 90, Family Church's fire was now blazing.

Do Family Church's impressive achievements tempt this church to rest on its laurels? To be content with its progress? Hardly. On the contrary, the leadership is focused and eager to challenge the congregation. And the congregation? They've caught the momentum and stepped up to a significant, risky move into the unknown—specifically to launch a new church campus.

"There's lots of unity and there's lots of excitement about where we're going," Ed reports. "And we are excited to see what God will do through Family Church as we allow him to accomplish his work through us."

THE HOPE FOR THE VIBRANT CHURCH

"Let's bust down the walls of this church!" So says Jeff Baker, senior pastor of New Life Church in Kearney, Nebraska, excited by his vision of planting life-giving church communities via video technology throughout rural America. New Life's first official church plant opened its doors in North Platte in October 2014.

This is the hope for all those who want the impact of Christ's gospel and Kingdom to grow: that a Vibrant Church like New Life would "bust down its walls" and spread its DNA like a spiritual wildfire.

Uniquely among the archetypes, the Vibrant Church possesses massive "spiritual capital," meaning it has a richness of spiritual resources available for the expansion of powerful ministry. Among those resources is the highest percentage of Christ-Centered congregants of all the archetypes—which translates into having the highest percentage of sacrificial servants, donors, and evangelists. The Vibrant Church also enjoys the strongest "platform of permission" (see chapter 7), built on the congregation's great love for the church and high regard for its leaders. The combination of this depth of spiritual maturity and the congregation's extraordinary goodwill toward the church makes planting Vibrant Churches anywhere and everywhere possibly the greatest opportunity for Christ's church today.

TROUBLED

COMPLACENT

EXTROVERTED

AVERAGE

INTROVERTED

SELF-MOTIVATED

ENERGIZED

VIBRANT

Unfortunately, not all Vibrant Churches may seize this opportunity because there is no sense of urgency. They are not losing congregants; in fact, their numbers are growing. And the truth is—there's an undeniable downside. Mark Ashton, senior pastor of Omaha's now-vibrant Christ Community Church, brings that downside to life with his story:

In April of 2008, Phil came to talk with me. He was the director of our high school and young adult ministries and a ten-year veteran of the church. "Mark," he said. "I think God is calling me to plant a church [awkward pause] . . . in Omaha. I am wondering how you would feel about it."

Losing an all-star veteran staff member feels like a punch in the gut, even if it is God's will. Although I hated to lose Phil, I knew that our church of three thousand could never reach a city of nine hundred thousand without multiplying. So I found myself choking out the words, "Even if you planted right next door to Christ Community, I'd support you." We gave Phil money, some time on stage to cast his vision, and—most importantly—a "fishing license" to take as many of our congregants with him as he could recruit. A year later, he took a hundred and twenty people and planted a church about twenty minutes away, in Gretna.

Then, in 2010, Purbha, a recent immigrant who was a godly lay leader, came to me and said, "I love everything about this church . . . except that you speak English." He wanted to take the forty Nepali-Bhutanese refugees who attended our church and create a church to reach their community—the only such church in Omaha. We blessed him, licensed him, gave him some money, and let him go.

But the biggest challenge took place in 2012, when our college pastor, who was also our second teaching pastor, said he wanted to plant a church. He was wildly charismatic, had lived in Nebraska his whole life, and had all of his spiritual roots at our church. But we gave him stage time, money, and a fishing license. Three hundred people joined him in a church plant about fifteen minutes away.

It hurts to give birth. In church terms, the rooms are a little emptier; budgets are a little leaner. Relationships get broken up. But mostly it hurts because you lose great leaders, evangelists, servants, and people you dearly love. But giving birth has a huge upside too.

Today, in 2014,

- Journey Church in Gretna has four hundred people attending—many of whom Christ Community Church never would have reached.
- New Life Church serves one hundred and fifty Nepali-Bhutanese refugees, and most have come to Christ in the last two years.
- CityLight Church has twelve hundred attenders from all over the city, radical conversion stories, and lots of young leaders who may never have set foot in an established church.

And Christ Community has grown by three hundred people, despite giving many away.

Spiritual capital. The hope for the Vibrant Church is that it will recognize the incredible spiritual wealth and great Kingdom potential at its disposal. And that it will risk the "punch in the gut" required to spend that capital to spread its church DNA throughout the country. The hope and prayer for the Vibrant Church is that it will become a role model, showing all archetypes how to open doors so that the Spirit, who "gives life," will be able to give it in accelerating abundance.

TROUBLED

COMPLACENT

EXTROVERTED

AVERAGE

INTROVERTED

SELF-MOTIVATED

ENERGIZED

VIBRANT

Symptoms of a Vibrant Church

A church likely falls into the Vibrant Church archetype if these three primary characteristics exist:

1. *Growth defines the church*—in numbers and in spiritual depth. Pastors see the numbers rising in all areas of church engagement, but also sense God's movement among congregants independent of church activities. People are on track with a spiritual quest to know and serve Christ, not only in partnership with the church but also on their own.
2. *Congregant approval is sky-high* for church direction, decisions, and leadership. Pastors can count on widespread support regardless of the church initiative being pursued. Feedback from congregants is almost always supportive, constructive, and encouraging.
3. *Challenge marks the culture*, demonstrated by authentic leadership role models. Pastors are well aware that they serve as role models for a fully surrendered life, often publicly acknowledging their spiritual shortfalls. Pastors also lead by example, showing up on the front line of all significant initiatives.

FAMILY CHURCH: 2014 UPDATE

What's the single biggest difference in Family Church since the case study?

After its second REVEAL survey, Family Church decided it had sufficient "spiritual capital" to launch its first regional campus. The church made some difficult financial decisions to ensure that a strong foundation was in place. For example, they remodeled existing facilities instead of building new ones so they could afford to start with a full-time campus pastor and two part-time assistants. Family Church's Green Campus opened its doors on Easter Sunday 2013.

What's new in Family Church discipleship strategies and culture since the case study?

The biggest discipleship change is a push to give birth to informal "quads/triads" out of their very strong small group system. The strategy is organic—simply an encouragement for congregants to meet once a month outside of the curriculum-based small group structure, with two or three like-minded Christ followers for unscripted reflection and greater accountability.

What's next on the horizon for Family Church?

Leaders felt that the launch of the Green Campus drew attention away from the church's four-stage discipleship pathway: Seeker, Student, Servant, and Steward. So they reinforced the pathway in the fall of 2014 with a "Journey Map" series designed to help congregants reengage with the stages of growth, and—more importantly—to self-identify their own spiritual maturity status and their most productive next steps. The hope is that this series (which asks people to create a spiritual growth "action plan"), in combination with the newly formed quads/triads, will set the stage for increased spiritual accountability and momentum. Once leaders are certain that the financial—and the spiritual—foundation for success is in place, Family Church also plans to launch additional campuses.

TROUBLED

COMPLACENT

EXTROVERTED

AVERAGE

INTROVERTED

SELF-MOTIVATED

ENERGIZED

VIBRANT

THE THINGS REVEALED: PART II

"What's our best next step? What would you do if you were me?"

Through a decade of church consultations, workshops, and many "unofficial" encounters with pastors, we have heard these questions—literally these very same words—countless times.

Our response—to them and now to you—is this final perspective on what the REVEAL team has learned from the eight church archetypes. The truth is we believe that this closing chapter of *Rise* may be the culmination of God's agenda for everything discovered by REVEAL—because these insights have such great potential to give church leaders what they so desperately need. Which is hope. Real, practical, fact-based *hope* that there is a path—strategies that can lead to increased spiritual vitality—no matter which archetype best fits their church today.

Our sole caveat is to begin with a cautious and sincere reminder that we do not pretend to be capable of advising your own particular, individual church. Only you and your fellow leaders, in concert with God's wisdom and mercy, can truly discern the best "next step" to help your people grow closer to Christ.

What we *can* do is provide you with a menu of options that have proven successful at creating spiritual velocity, based on numerous consultations with churches that have advanced in spiritual maturity between multiple REVEAL surveys. These "next steps" will be delivered in two ways. First, because you are undoubtedly most anxious to understand the pathway applicable to your particular archetype, we will start by covering those customized pathways in a somewhat abbreviated manner. Then we will step back and provide comprehensive descriptions of the fifteen strategies used to assemble those pathways.

THE PATHWAYS FOR THE ARCHETYPES

Based on consultations with hundreds of pastors leading churches that have demonstrated spiritual progress, we offer fifteen strategies that have the greatest spiritual growth potential. This list is not meant to be exhaustive, because—as you can imagine—talking with hundreds of creative pastors has generated an extensive inventory of ideas. Instead, this list captures the strategies that occur repeatedly in churches showing statistically meaningful evidence of spiritual momentum.

These top strategies for advancing spiritual growth, categorized according to the five Best Practice Principles introduced in chapter 1, are as follows:

HOW TO "GET PEOPLE MOVING":

1. The Alpha Course
2. The Purpose Driven "Baseball Diamond"
3. A Defined Discipleship Pathway

HOW TO "EMBED THE BIBLE IN EVERYTHING":

4. Integrated, High-Profile Bible-Based Campaigns
5. Spiritual Role Models and Reminders
6. Spiritual Mentoring

HOW TO "CREATE OWNERSHIP":

7. Small Group Build-Up
8. "Living It" Campaigns
9. Lay Leaders with Big Jobs

HOW TO "PASTOR THE LOCAL COMMUNITY":

10. Unconventional Servant Leadership Vision
11. Partnerships with Local Officials, Nonprofits, and Churches
12. Community Service Investment

HOW TO DEMONSTRATE "CHRIST-CENTERED LEADERSHIP":

13. Ruthless Reality Check
14. "Your First Love" Recharge
15. Spiritual Capital Assessment

You will find a comprehensive, in-depth description of these strategies in the next section of this chapter.[1] But first, here are the high-impact pathways for each of the eight archetypes, based on an assessment of the *top three strategies* most likely to create spiritual traction.

Starting with the Troubled Church, Chart 10.1 illustrates the journey that lies ahead—which is the longest and most difficult road to spiritual vitality of all the archetypes.

---

[1] A full description of the fifteen strategies and the best practices they represent can be found on pages 163–174.

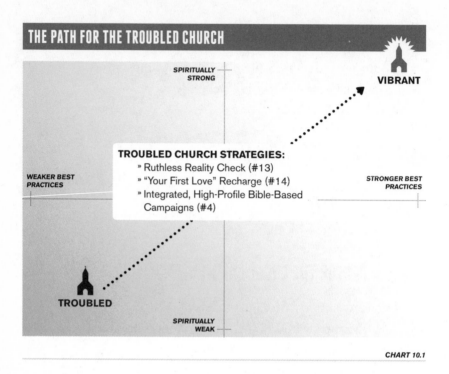

THE PATH FOR THE TROUBLED CHURCH

SPIRITUALLY STRONG

VIBRANT

TROUBLED CHURCH STRATEGIES:
» Ruthless Reality Check (#13)
» "Your First Love" Recharge (#14)
» Integrated, High-Profile Bible-Based Campaigns (#4)

WEAKER BEST PRACTICES

STRONGER BEST PRACTICES

TROUBLED

SPIRITUALLY WEAK

CHART 10.1

The hope for the Troubled Church rests with the courage of its leaders to confront the reality of an unhappy, spiritually immature congregation. The three strategies most likely to overcome those challenges are listed on Chart 10.1 in order of priority. The first step is an unemotional, objective evaluation of the church's circumstances—paying special attention to the competency of leaders in the positions required for the turnaround it needs. The introduction of a campaign to recharge the church's spiritual batteries is also a logical step, one that could be taken simultaneously.

The biggest issue for the next archetype, the Complacent Church, is its deeply rooted spiritual apathy. Unlike the Troubled Church, it benefits from a positive, albeit passive, relationship with its congregation—which makes its road easier, although it still faces a difficult climb from spiritual indifference to vitality (see Chart 10.2).

The hope for the Complacent Church is a spiritual boost from

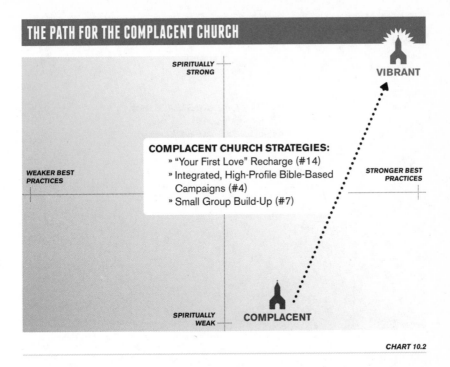

THE PATH FOR THE COMPLACENT CHURCH

SPIRITUALLY STRONG

VIBRANT

COMPLACENT CHURCH STRATEGIES:
» "Your First Love" Recharge (#14)
» Integrated, High-Profile Bible-Based Campaigns (#4)
» Small Group Build-Up (#7)

WEAKER BEST PRACTICES

STRONGER BEST PRACTICES

SPIRITUALLY WEAK

COMPLACENT

CHART 10.2

a coordinated set of strategies that will unite the church body in a fun, interactive experience with the Bible. However, like most of the archetypes, the journey starts with leadership. We recall a comment by a Complacent Church pastor when clear signs of progress began to emerge: "I think they sensed my excitement and just caught it!" That's where it starts—with fired-up, spiritually refreshed leaders.

The Extroverted Church faces a very different challenge, which is to take some of the enthusiasm its congregants bring to community outreach and redirect it to Bible engagement—without losing their passion for those in need (see Chart 10.3).

The hope for the Extroverted Church is that the goodwill congregants feel toward the church and its leaders will pave the way for wide acceptance of spiritual jump-start strategies such as Alpha. An emphasis on spiritual role models, including congregant testimonies about "God encounters," might balance their current serving experiences

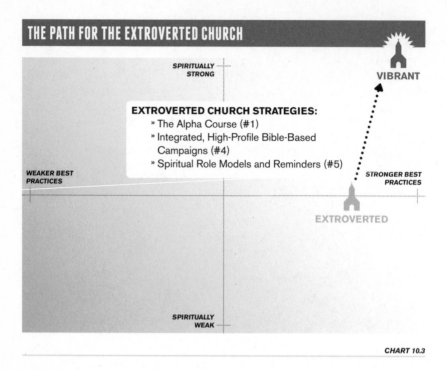

THE PATH FOR THE EXTROVERTED CHURCH

SPIRITUALLY STRONG

VIBRANT

EXTROVERTED CHURCH STRATEGIES:
» The Alpha Course (#1)
» Integrated, High-Profile Bible-Based Campaigns (#4)
» Spiritual Role Models and Reminders (#5)

WEAKER BEST PRACTICES

STRONGER BEST PRACTICES

EXTROVERTED

SPIRITUALLY WEAK

CHART 10.3

with ones that are more reflective and Scripture-based. The future of Extroverted Churches is very bright, once their roots of faith are planted more firmly in God's presence and power.

The challenge for the Average Church, on the other hand, is less about motivating congregants to deepen their faith—and more about church leaders revisiting and reawakening their hearts for God's work (see Chart 10.4).

All three strategies depend on church leaders taking the initiative to reflect and recharge their discipleship spirit. A great start would be to assemble a group of trusted spiritual leaders to discern their collective point of view about a pathway for discipleship—then to activate a plan to communicate it to the church's congregants.

Another archetype that would gain traction from a defined discipleship path is the Introverted Church, which is in a very strong position to make spiritual headway (see Chart 10.5).

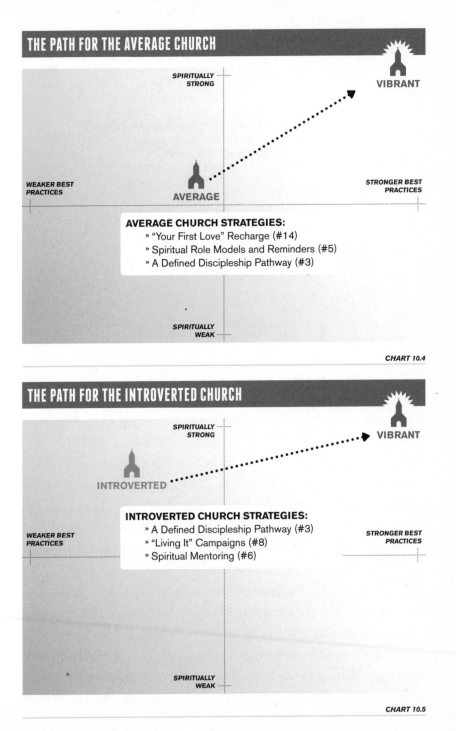

THE PATH FOR THE AVERAGE CHURCH

SPIRITUALLY STRONG

VIBRANT

WEAKER BEST PRACTICES

AVERAGE

STRONGER BEST PRACTICES

AVERAGE CHURCH STRATEGIES:
» "Your First Love" Recharge (#14)
» Spiritual Role Models and Reminders (#5)
» A Defined Discipleship Pathway (#3)

SPIRITUALLY WEAK

CHART 10.4

THE PATH FOR THE INTROVERTED CHURCH

SPIRITUALLY STRONG

VIBRANT

INTROVERTED

INTROVERTED CHURCH STRATEGIES:
» A Defined Discipleship Pathway (#3)
» "Living It" Campaigns (#8)
» Spiritual Mentoring (#6)

WEAKER BEST PRACTICES

STRONGER BEST PRACTICES

SPIRITUALLY WEAK

CHART 10.5

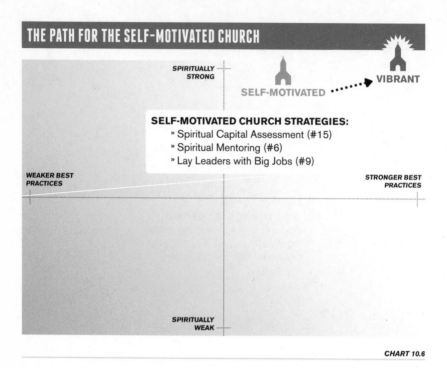

THE PATH FOR THE SELF-MOTIVATED CHURCH

SPIRITUALLY STRONG

VIBRANT

SELF-MOTIVATED

SELF-MOTIVATED CHURCH STRATEGIES:
» Spiritual Capital Assessment (#15)
» Spiritual Mentoring (#6)
» Lay Leaders with Big Jobs (#9)

WEAKER BEST PRACTICES

STRONGER BEST PRACTICES

SPIRITUALLY WEAK

CHART 10.6

Congregants attending an Introverted Church already enjoy a lifestyle that incorporates their faith into their daily lives. The hope is that this strong spiritual foundation sets them up to react favorably and immediately to a new awareness about discipleship expectations, which a defined pathway will create. "Living it" campaigns and spiritual mentoring would be excellent reinforcement strategies.

Spiritual mentoring is, in fact, one of the top three strategies for the Self-Motivated Church, which also benefits from a congregation with deep spiritual roots (see Chart 10.6).

These faith-filled congregants, however, seem somewhat disengaged from the church, feeling perhaps that its discipleship fervor has waned. The most essential strategy for a church within this archetype is a candid assessment of its spiritual capital. Since that assessment will likely show signs of erosion, it will be important to take steps to restore congregant confidence in a church vision centered on Christ. Using its

THE PATH FOR THE ENERGIZED CHURCH

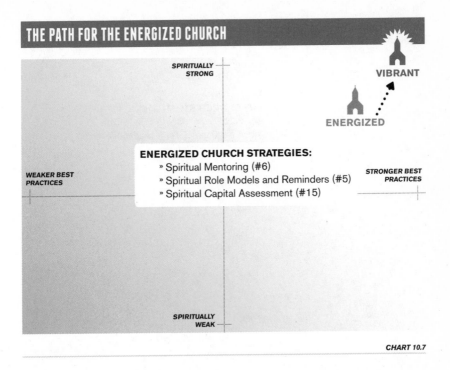

SPIRITUALLY STRONG

VIBRANT

ENERGIZED

ENERGIZED CHURCH STRATEGIES:
» Spiritual Mentoring (#6)
» Spiritual Role Models and Reminders (#5)
» Spiritual Capital Assessment (#15)

WEAKER BEST PRACTICES

STRONGER BEST PRACTICES

SPIRITUALLY WEAK

CHART 10.7

plentiful reserves of mature Christ followers to recruit lay leaders for significant ministry positions might help with that restoration.

The Energized Church is the closest of all the archetypes to the Vibrant Church. Spiritual mentoring could be the key to its final advance (see Chart 10.7).

In combination with spiritual mentoring, an enhanced strategy to use role modeling to reinforce what a life centered on Jesus looks like would strengthen the faith of these congregants, as well as fortify their already-deep appreciation for the church. The Energized Church should also keep an eye on its spiritual capital, because it is poised for high-impact ministry expansion and investment.

Although we can plot no visual path for the Vibrant Church, the very nature of its spiritual character means it is always learning, always advancing. No Vibrant Church would suggest that it has arrived at an "ideal" discipleship destination (see Chart 10.8).

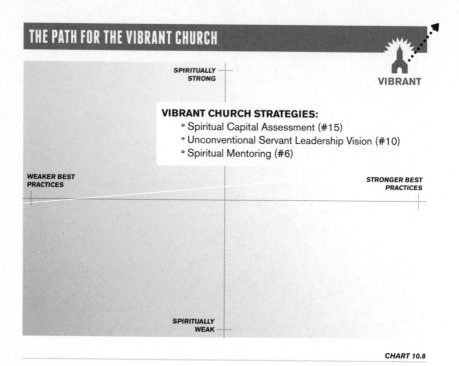

THE PATH FOR THE VIBRANT CHURCH

SPIRITUALLY STRONG

VIBRANT

VIBRANT CHURCH STRATEGIES:
» Spiritual Capital Assessment (#15)
» Unconventional Servant Leadership Vision (#10)
» Spiritual Mentoring (#6)

WEAKER BEST PRACTICES

STRONGER BEST PRACTICES

SPIRITUALLY WEAK

CHART 10.8

The hope for the Vibrant Church is the hope for us all—that it will invest its abundant spiritual capital in creative and compelling expansion initiatives. That could include a strategy to take up the mantle of servant leadership, which may have global as well as local implications. Since these external spiritual investments will sap time and energy, the introduction of a mentoring strategy would help ensure that the spiritual reserves of the Vibrant Church stay replenished.

✦ ✦ ✦

So now, you have our answer to that ever-present, recurring "What's my next step?" question asked by pastors everywhere. These archetype pathways are our best response, based on everything we've learned in ten years of research with more than two thousand churches and hundreds of thousands of congregants.

We close this section about archetype pathways by acknowledging that they are admittedly imperfect and incomplete. Imperfect, because every church has its own strengths and weaknesses—so a cookie-cutter set of "next steps" provides less of a prepackaged solution for church leaders than simply food for thought. In that spirit, we hope you'll read through the expanded descriptions of all fifteen strategies that follow, to continue your quest to determine the most effective strategies for your church.

These pathways also remain incomplete, because God continues to refresh our inventory of "things revealed" (Deuteronomy 29:29). We will continue to fulfill our accountability to him—and to you—by communicating the most discipleship-worthy strategies that cross our path. We hope you will likewise pursue an ongoing process to discern what the "things revealed" can mean to you and your church.

FIFTEEN STRATEGIES THAT LEAD TO BEST PRACTICES

Chapter 1 briefly described the five Best Practice Principles that help churches advance their congregants' spiritual growth, and at the beginning of this chapter we briefly reviewed those best practices. In this section, you will find a more comprehensive point of view about how these best practices work, and the fifteen strategies that churches pursue to bring them to life.

We cannot claim the ideas that follow are statistically infallible—in other words, we cannot be certain they will drive spiritual growth in any church, including yours. We are confident, however, that they are worthy of prayerful consideration by all church leaders who want the "lamp" of God's Word and the "light" of His love to guide the lives of their people.

Best Practice Principle #1: How to "Get People Moving"

This is the ignition-switch strategy for making sure newcomers and veteran churchgoers alike are crystal clear about the "first steps" you want them to pursue, as well as your point of view about what a spiritual journey looks like. These three options have the potential to deliver a spiritual jump-start that challenges the soul and opens the door for the Spirit to transform the heart:

1. The Alpha Course

This blockbuster global Christian course would almost certainly be on the top-ten list of independent initiatives most effective at helping people decide to put their faith in Jesus Christ. Created originally in 1977 by a Church of England parish as a course for new believers, it soon became a ten-week interactive experience for nonbelievers. The curriculum was extensively revised in the early 1990s by Nicky Gumbel, and since then, an estimated twenty million people worldwide have attended Alpha classes, impacting virtually all branches of Christianity. Many of the most impressive REVEAL churches use Alpha as a next step for the "faith fence-sitters" in their congregation.

2. The Purpose Driven "Baseball Diamond"

Probably the best-known Christian orientation model for church newcomers, this four-stage process starts with a church leader—ideally the senior pastor—describing the vision and values of the church. Subsequent sessions connect people with the church's fellowship networks (often small groups), introduce the concept of personal spiritual practices, and assess how people might use their spiritual gifts to serve the church. Many Vibrant Churches provide an orientation path that reflects the influence of the Purpose Driven model, which is heavily promoted as the next step for newcomers.

3. A Defined Discipleship Pathway

For years, churches have provided pathways leading to spiritual growth. But most have focused on "what to do" to grow spiritually—with an emphasis on participating in church activities like small groups, serving in a church ministry, and regularly attending worship services.

Many churches that have demonstrated significant spiritual gains report using some version of the REVEAL Spiritual Continuum as their discipleship pathway. This may work because it adds the "why" behind the "what"—in other words, it reinforces the principle that the goal of the activities is to help people connect with God and develop an increasingly mature relationship with Christ. It may also demystify the spiritual journey by providing concrete definitions for the different stages of maturity. In any event, the research shows that defining and communicating your preferred point of view about a discipleship pathway and its destination (for example, becoming Christ-Centered), can fuel spiritual energy in your church.

Best Practice Principle #2:
How to "Embed the Bible in Everything"

Possibly the best-known and highest-impact finding from REVEAL is that reflecting on Scripture "for meaning in my life" is *by far* the most powerful catalyst of spiritual growth. Bible engagement statistics, however, show disappointing numbers about how rarely even longtime churchgoers open their Bibles. Only 20 percent of congregants on average—and often single-digit percentages in individual churches—read Scripture every day.

Regardless of archetype, when the frequency of Bible engagement rises, spiritual momentum abounds. The following three options have proven themselves highly effective at helping those numbers increase:

4. Integrated, High-Profile Bible-Based Campaigns

This may be the most effective spiritual growth strategy we've uncovered. A typical campaign unifies the curriculum for teaching and study across a church's most significant activities, including weekend services, small groups, and children's ministry. As implied by the word *campaign*, these initiatives normally continue for six weeks or longer. Two examples of curriculums used successfully by many churches are Scripture Union's E100 program, which challenges a church body to read five Bible stories each week for twenty weeks, and Zondervan's *The Story*, which covers Genesis to Revelation in chronological order over a ministry season. These campaigns almost universally generate enthusiasm and spiritual cohesion within a church body. A pastor of a Vibrant Church near Atlanta recently described the positive response of his congregation to Saddleback's *40 Days in the Word*, another campaign option, as "overwhelming."

The power of this integrated campaign strategy may be derived from two consistent elements: first, the appeal of its very focused challenge; and second, its limited scope, which makes it a proposition that people can fit into their lives.

5. Spiritual Role Models and Reminders

It goes without saying that Bible-based teaching is a prerequisite for a spiritually vibrant culture. But the highly visible teaching platform is, almost more importantly, the place where people expect to see spiritual growth and maturity come to life. In fact, REVEAL research shows that one of the most important functions of the senior pastor is to "model and reinforce how to grow spiritually."

Senior pastors in the strongest churches model spiritual practices as disciplines that are ingrained in their daily lives—meaning that they are immersed in Scripture, deriving direction from God's Word and through prayer. Many top churches take this role modeling a step beyond the teaching platform, providing fresh insights about key Scriptures throughout the week via e-mail, text messages, and/or tweets.

A practical tool used by many pastors to encourage and equip their congregations in spiritual practices is the well-known SOAP process developed by Wayne Cordeiro, senior pastor of New Hope

Oahu. It encourages individuals to spend time in Scripture every day, capturing Observations, Applications, and Prayers in a Life Journal designed for this purpose.

But there is no "silver bullet" program that provides instructions on how to be a spiritual role model—or identifies which reminders about spiritual engagement will have the greatest impact. However, there's no better investment of time and energy for church leaders than to figure out what sort of strategy will work in their church culture. That's because the deeper the REVEAL team digs into the research, the more convinced we become that personal spiritual practices—in particular, reflection on Scripture—drive everything.

6. Spiritual Mentoring

It is not surprising that even the most mature Christ followers plateau, at times, in their spiritual development. That's not to say they "stall," but they can coast. Given the ample evidence regarding the underchallenged nature of the Christ-Centered segment (for example, only half of them have more than six spiritual conversations with nonbelievers in a year), a spiritual coaching strategy clearly designed for them would be helpful. Fortunately, such a strategy exists in a number of Vibrant Churches.

As described in chapter 8, spiritual mentoring in stronger churches is more of an organic process than a ministry. It begins with the senior pastor and/or church leadership staff, who mentor a few leaders, typically using a standardized curriculum such as the Navigators 2:7 Series or Regi Campbell's Radical Mentoring program. Those who are mentored are then expected to mentor others, but there is no "official" recruiting, so awareness of the opportunity spreads mostly by word of mouth.

We've also discovered several in-depth discipleship initiatives that are close cousins to spiritual mentoring but follow a distinctly different format. While the mentoring process is relatively informal and often limited to two or three participants, these programs are more like classes that are publicly championed at the church. For example, the Warm Beach Free Methodist Church case study in chapter 7 cited Disciple Road, a very demanding one-year commitment limited to a group of twenty people. The launch of this curriculum likely was the most significant influence on Warm Beach's improved SVI.

Another high-impact curriculum is Christian Leadership Concepts (CLC). Like Disciple Road, it's a demanding curriculum, requiring two hours each week for class time, with several more dedicated to homework. Unlike Disciple Road, the program lasts two years, and the participation is gender-specific and confined to twelve participants. The pastor of a church in Ohio described the success of CLC as "astounding to me." Launched with limited fanfare, more than 20 percent of his church's male congregants have thus far committed to the program.

The influence on a church's spiritual vitality of these strategies—the in-depth discipleship courses and the mentoring process—goes well beyond the impact on the participants themselves. The awareness that such efforts are supported and made available by the church speaks volumes to its most mature congregants. In fact, the Ohio church shifted from the Self-Motivated to the Vibrant Church archetype in its latest survey—probably as a direct result of its discipleship curriculum.

Best Practice Principle #3: How to "Create Ownership"

Connection and *community* may be somewhat overused words in church life, but those two concepts lie at the heart of strategies designed to create ownership. This best practice, which strives to knit together the relational soul of the congregation, is activated by the following three most effective strategies:

7. Small Group Build-Up

To be clear, small groups are a means to an end. In other words, building a small group network is not a purposeful goal unless there is a clearly articulated role it will serve. The most effective role REVEAL has uncovered is that of a community network put in place to support specific church initiatives, such as the Bible-based campaigns noted earlier. In fact, it is through those campaigns that small groups are most likely to grow and expand. For example, one church in Georgia reported that its small groups more than tripled—from thirty to ninety-four—during a fall ministry campaign. The groups did decline during similar initiatives in the winter and spring, but only to seventy—still more than double the original number.

Beyond the campaign strategy, two additional factors contribute to building up small groups. The first is to offer a physical space, ideally the church building, for small group meetings during the week. Establishing this central hub makes it possible to provide free or low-cost childcare, which is often the major obstacle to small group success.

8. "Living It" Campaigns

Some of the most effective "living it" campaigns involve money. For example, a Vibrant Church in New Jersey distributed sealed envelopes containing undisclosed amounts of cash to congregants, along with a challenge to listen for the Holy Spirit's prompting about the cause or person most deserving of the money. Stories flooded in about miraculous "matches" of needs and the dollar amounts in the envelopes, reinforcing the power of staying attuned to spiritual whispers.

When another church's fund-raising campaign fell short of what was needed for their support of an African hospital, a similar initiative developed. They distributed $20,000 to congregants with the challenge to multiply it. The resulting 5K runs, golf outings, yoga classes, and lemonade stands raised $438,000—and created the opportunity for many spiritual conversations with nonchurched neighbors and friends.

These classic "living it" strategies encourage people to break out of their comfort zones and experiment with faith-related behaviors, such as listening for the Holy Spirit's voice, interacting with and serving those in need, and evangelizing. Preempting weekend services for community outreach is another strategy used by many churches to create similar "living it" opportunities. The key is to inspire people to engage in a new faith-based behavior outside the walls of the church, so that the behavior might become more common in their daily lives.

9. Lay Leaders with Big Jobs

This strategy is a win-win for spiritual growth and church operations. The concept is to position lay leaders in significant and highly visible ministry positions, similar to Bob Wine (chapter 8's New Life case study), who tapped a trusted congregant to serve as the spiritual matchmaker for their church's mentoring process. This idea goes beyond appointing volunteer lay people to a church board of elders. It is a strategy to flag highly visible and critical functions that may not require seminary training—like finance, human resources, communications, or community outreach—and invite congregants to step into those roles before turning to people with ministry experience.

Given the current demographic swell of retiring, "empty nest" baby-boomer professionals, significant resources are likely sitting in your church pews. In light of how often our follow-up telephone consultations include lay leaders with business expertise and backgrounds, it's clear that many churches are aware of and appreciate this opportunity. The benefit is twofold. Church operations add capabilities groomed in the public sector, at low to no cost. And the DNA of church vision becomes increasingly shared and shouldered by people who first came to the church to find God, not a paycheck.

Best Practice #4: How to "Pastor the Local Community"

The intentional use of the word *pastor* rather than *serve* captures the spirit of this best practice. To pastor is to shepherd, which implies engagement, guidance, and oversight. Churches that excel as such shepherds in their communities work arm-in-arm with local officials and nonprofits to do much more than serve. Their aspiration is to *solve* whatever problems plague their demographic footprint by partnering and pooling resources with others. Three strategies that accomplish this include:

10. Unconventional Servant Leadership Vision

This strategy is nothing short of a "change the world" agenda, starting with the immediate community footprint that surrounds the church. The concept is to make the essence of Christ's parable of the sheep and goats (see Matthew 25:31-46) the heartbeat of the church by providing constant opportunities for congregants to serve Jesus by meeting the needs of "the least of these." The positive impact will be felt by congregants on both ends of the Spiritual Continuum, as those on the sidelines of faith readily agree to join community service efforts and the most mature Christ followers use these initiatives as opportune occasions to share their faith.

The key to this vision's success—in terms of both spiritual and community impact—is the senior pastor's full endorsement and engagement, because it is his or her heart that will galvanize the rest of the hands and feet. Without the highest level of commitment from the leader of the church, the community may well be "served"—but it will not be saved or transformed.

11. Partnerships with Local Officials, Nonprofits, and Other Churches

This is by far the most effective strategy related to community outreach and impact. While we've seen wide variations of this strategy work well in different community settings, the centerpiece distinction is its spirit of hands-on, roll-up-the-sleeves humility. The key seems to be moving from a strategy of creating go-it-alone programs that address issues dear to the heart of church leaders to a strategy of working with local nonprofit networks to discover *their* most critical needs. The next step is to coalesce the resources and goodwill of others to remedy the problems at hand.

This can be a messy process, one replete with uncharted obstacles due to the need for working relationships with often unknown, secular organizations. But it seems to be the most likely way to achieve real transformation—not only in the community, but also within the lives of people both inside and outside the church body.

12. Community Service Investment

"Put your money where your mouth is" is a crass synopsis of this strategy, which means that significant ministry time, energy, and resources are required to affect real community transformation. Churches that do this successfully hire and/or recruit passionate individuals to focus all of their energies solely toward the creation of ongoing, creative community service opportunities. In addition, these positions are prominent and influential, often reporting directly to the senior pastor. Another effective strategy is to require all church staff members to join a local organization, such as the PTA or Chamber of Commerce, in order to keep a finger on the pulse of local concerns.

Best Practice #5:
How to Demonstrate "Christ-Centered Leadership"

"The buck stops here," was Harry Truman's motto, and it's as true in the church as it is in the presidency. While elder boards and other spiritual advisors surround and support most pastors, being the church standard-bearer is a tough position—doubly so, given that pastors shoulder the responsibility for modeling Christlike behavior in their every decision and interaction. While we cannot advise on how to navigate the internal dynamics of Christ-centered leadership, the following are three strategies that are often undertaken by leaders of spiritually strong churches:

13. Ruthless Reality Check

Any church would be well served to engage in an unvarnished, unfiltered review of its most promising opportunities to fulfill the Great Commission, and the most significant obstacles in its path. This strategy was described at length as the hope for the Troubled Church in chapter 2—but it's a healthy exercise for all churches to undergo on a regular basis. It involves three steps: first, an objective assessment of the discipleship character, chemistry, and competency of the leadership group; second, a refocus on the church's discipleship mission, sorting the ministry wheat (what's working) from the chaff (what's not); and third, a ruthless evaluation of what needs to be added or cut to achieve the church's greatest spiritual potential.

This is probably the biggest "miss" for organizations in general—and the church, in particular. It is our hope that *Rise*, through its eight archetypes, provides church leaders with new insights about the core issues this strategy addresses: their greatest opportunities, their most significant obstacles, and ideas about how to tackle them.

14. "Your First Love" Recharge

Love for Christ defines the very soul of a church, yet it doesn't always show up on the church staff meeting agenda, for two reasons. The first is understandable, which is that the drain of operational demands and distractions of ministry can overwhelm the capacity of leaders. Churches have much to accomplish, and staffing and budgets tend to run very lean. So carving out time to recharge church teams with a reminder of their shared love for Jesus may seem more discretionary than required.

The real danger, however, is the assumption by seasoned church leaders that people who have dedicated their lives to ministry will replenish their own spiritual reserves—so that to spend time during the ministry workweek to refresh a church staff's collective spirit is unnecessary, even a waste of time and money.

The list of ways to recharge "your first love" is endless—from simple steps, like including fifteen minutes for "God showed up!" stories at staff meetings, to regular spiritual staff retreats. The point is to make spiritual renewal as high a priority within church leadership circles as it is for weekend worship services.

15. Spiritual Capital Assessment

Similar to the business world, where decisions to expand product lines or markets depend on financial capital, churches should determine their expansion plans—whether that means increasing ministry capacity or church planting—based on their spiritual capital. This process depends on two factors. First, a church needs to assess its "platform of permission," as described in chapter 7. This relates to the goodwill extended to the church by its congregants. If they love the church, respect the senior pastor, and are highly supportive of the church vision, then they will cooperate and contribute to whatever initiative church leaders introduce. Spiritual capital also depends on the faith-based maturity of the congregation, because a strong spiritual foundation provides far more commitment and resources than one that is weak.

The implication is that churches should dedicate their resources to either building up their spiritual capital reserves if they are depleted—or investing those reserves aggressively to extend and expand their impact.

+ + +

Again, these fifteen strategies are admittedly imperfect—in other words, not a formula for spiritual success for every church—and incomplete, because we are confident God will disclose more "things revealed" through this work. But we offer them to you with great hope—hope that they will help you to lead more effectively, and that your leadership will inspire the church of Jesus Christ to *rise*.

"BUT WE'VE ALWAYS DONE IT THIS WAY!"

Nancy Scammacca Lewis

This is often the prototypical refrain when leaders want to introduce a change designed to move things in a better direction. We would be remiss if, in this chapter on strategies for changing your church, we didn't talk about how to navigate change and overcome the temptation to bail out when things get rough.

There is a phenomenon in organizational dynamics known as the "J-curve." Understanding it can make the difference between seeing a change through to the fulfillment of its promise or giving up and returning to the less-than-thriving status quo. The J-curve shows that during a change in programs, processes, or systems, it is normal for things to get worse before they get better.

As illustrated in Chart 10.9, at the beginning of the change process, a church is achieving a certain level of results with the status quo. When a change process gets underway, there is often a period of decline—a "valley" phase—when people complain, things seem worse than they were before, and many say, "This isn't working." The decline can be due to the time it takes congregants to accept a new program, or the effort required to get to know and trust a new staff member hired to oversee the change process. Sometimes the valley represents a natural adjustment period, as everyone struggles to get comfortable with a new way of doing things.

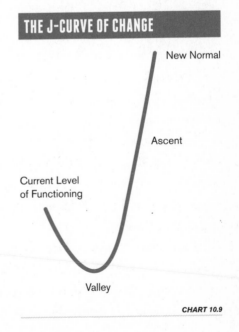

THE J-CURVE OF CHANGE

New Normal

Ascent

Current Level
of Functioning

Valley

CHART 10.9

I served on the pastoral staff of a church during just such an adjustment period. Our Sunday attendance had mushroomed from one hundred to three hundred in eighteen months; the church had outgrown our rented worship space and needed to move to a new location. It also had outgrown systems that worked well when the congregation was small. In particular, the ministry volunteer scheduling system now lacked the capacity to handle the congregation's needs. Tasked with implementing a new system that would accommodate future growth in the congregation, I chose a web-based scheduler that would centralize and automate the process. Because our new location required adjustments to many of our serving teams, we timed the change to coincide with our move.

We worked hard to get our team leaders on board—and to communicate what we were doing and why to all of our volunteers. I prepared step-by-step guides to walk even the most technophobic congregants through the process of enrolling in the online system. But despite multiple reminders sent to ministry volunteers to log into the system and set up their preferences, once the system went live and the automated scheduling e-mails went out, the complaints began rolling in. After a couple of days of dealing with upset team leaders and frustrated congregants, our senior pastor threw up his hands, saying, "This is a disaster!" That's when I knew we had reached the J-curve's valley.

The leadership decisions made during this critical phase of the change process are key to changing a church's direction. Bailing out will silence the critics but will also undermine credibility moving forward. The next time you launch a new initiative or try a new strategy, the congregation may be less likely to believe that you mean to see it through. Moreover, going back to the way things were means settling for the church's previous lackluster results.

Two simple (but not easy) action steps are key to successfully navigating the bottom of the J-curve. First, anticipate the inevitability of the valley. Acknowledge that there may be some resistance—and that initially, the new strategy might not seem to work. You and your key leaders should be prepared for pushback.

Second, cast vision for where this change will take the church. Talk about the goal of the new strategy as often and with as many people as possible. Coach leaders to do the same and support them as they absorb some of the heat. Take every opportunity to cast vision for the life-giving results that will ensue. When you start to see those results, celebrate them publicly. Tell stories about how the change is making a difference. Soon, the congregation's morale will lift your church into the "ascent" stage of the J-curve, where the hard work pays off for everyone.

Successfully navigating one change cycle builds momentum for the next change, encouraging people to follow you through what likely will be a shorter J-curve journey. That is exactly what happened at my church once our senior pastor understood that the "disaster" of the new scheduling system was a normal part of change. (It became even clearer as frustrations were expressed with other changes taking place at our growing church—from the loss of intimacy to parking issues.) In response, he wrote a blog post explaining the J-curve and casting vision for the goal of the changes: to help more lost and broken people connect to Christ and his community. Our pastor used the pulpit to reinforce that message and encouraged church leaders to hang in there while we worked out the bugs. That was more than four years ago, and since then the church has doubled in size—growth that would not have been possible had we failed to press on through the pain of the J-curve to implement changes in support of our church's mission.

RESEARCH APPROACH AND METHODOLOGY

As the REVEAL team surveyed more and more churches and had countless conversations with their leaders, patterns emerged that reflected similarities between them. Over time, we began to name and describe these patterns. When we knew we had data on enough churches to determine if these patterns would rise to the surface when tested statistically, we began our analysis. Chapter 1 provided a conceptual overview of the qualitative and quantitative process of discovering the archetypes; in this appendix, we provide a more detailed and technical look at the statistical methods used in that process for those who are interested in a deeper dive into the quantitative procedures behind the findings presented in *Rise*.

WHO ARE THE 727 CHURCHES?

The statistical findings about the archetypes in *Rise* are based on 727 churches surveyed between 2008 and 2010. We chose this time frame because churches that participated prior to September 2008 responded to an earlier version of the survey that lacked some items considered critically important to identifying the patterns that ultimately became the archetypes. The demographic tables provided here profile this dataset of churches, showing its breadth and diversity. We included all churches that responded to the REVEAL survey. No weighting or redistribution was done to attempt to balance the sample or create a particular demographic profile.

GEOGRAPHIC LOCATION OF THE 727 CHURCHES

GEOGRAPHIC REGION	GEOGRAPHIC SECTION	PERCENTAGE OF THE 727 CHURCHES
Northeast	New England	2%
	Middle Atlantic	8%
Midwest	East North Central	32%
	West North Central	7%
South	South Atlantic	14%
	East South Central	4%
	West South Central	11%
West	Mountain	6%
	Pacific	12%
Canada	Alberta	2%
	Ontario	1%
	Other	2%

COMMUNITY TYPE OF THE 727 CHURCHES

COMMUNITY TYPE	PERCENTAGE OF THE 727 CHURCHES
Rural or open country	19%
Suburban	68%
Urban	12%

WEEKEND ADULT ATTENDANCE OF THE 727 CHURCHES

AVERAGE WEEKEND ADULT ATTENDANCE	PERCENTAGE OF THE 727 CHURCHES
Less than 100	4%
100–249	28%
250–499	25%
500–999	30%
1,000–2,499	11%
2,500–4,999	2%
5,000 or more	1%

DENOMINATIONS REPRESENTED IN THE 727 CHURCHES

CHURCH DENOMINATION	PERCENTAGE OF THE 727 CHURCHES
Nondenominational	26%
Baptist	14%
Methodist	10%
Lutheran	10%
Presbyterian/Reformed	7%
Christian/Church of Christ	5%
Assembly of God/Church of God/Pentecostal	4%
Evangelical Free	3%
Brethren	2%
Christian and Missionary Alliance	2%
Evangelical Covenant	2%
Wesleyan	2%
Other	13%

STEP ONE: CONFIRMATORY FACTOR ANALYSIS

In 2010, the REVEAL team set out to analyze the database of 727 churches. As we embarked on the quantitative analysis, two frameworks guided our work: the Best Practice Principles and the Spiritual Growth Catalysts (see chapter 1, pages 3–7 for a description of these).

Our first step was to identify items on the REVEAL survey that measured each principle and catalyst. Using inter-item correlation matrices, we reduced the list of items pertaining to each principle and catalyst to those with the highest intercorrelations. Then we conducted separate confirmatory factor analyses (CFAs) for the catalysts and the Best Practice Principles to determine which items best fit each construct and comprised a valid overall model of the relationships among the principles and among the catalysts. The final lists consisted of three to four items per principle or catalyst, all of which had loadings of 0.60 or higher on their corresponding factor. Fit indices for both measurement models indicated that the models had excellent fit for the data, with moderate correlations between principles and between catalysts in each model.

STEP TWO: K-MEANS CLUSTER ANALYSIS

Using the items identified in the CFAs, the churches in our dataset were given percentile ranks for their average scores for the set of items used to measure each principle and catalyst. This percentile rank represented the church's level of effectiveness in each area relative to all of the other churches in the dataset. For example, a church with a score of 25 on Get People Moving delivers this principle at a level that is higher than 25 percent of the churches in the database. A church with a score of 72 on Beliefs ranked higher on that catalyst than 72 percent of churches.

Using these percentile ranks, we ran a K-means cluster analysis to group churches based on these variables. We analyzed the catalysts and Best Practice Principles separately. Beginning with the Best Practice Principles, we tried as few as three clusters and as many as nine clusters. For each solution, we compared the results for the clusters of churches on items from the REVEAL survey that measure personal spiritual practices, beliefs, church activities, satisfaction with the church's role in spiritual growth, faith-in-action behaviors, and other key items. Our goal was to find a solution that included only groups that are distinct from one another in ways that are meaningful in defining the archetype in each cluster. A five-group clustering solution achieved these criteria for the Best Practice Principles. Table A.1 shows how the groups compared.

CLUSTERING BASED ON THE BEST PRACTICE PRINCIPLES

PERCENTILE RANK:	CLUSTER 1	CLUSTER 2	CLUSTER 3	CLUSTER 4	CLUSTER 5
Get People Moving	15	22	48	74	84
Embed the Bible	19	71	50	25	75
Create Ownership	18	19	48	80	81
Pastor the Community	18	21	47	77	81

TABLE A.1

Overall, this framework felt incomplete. More than a third of churches in our dataset fell into the "average" cluster (Cluster 3), but it seemed like there were multiple types of churches in this cluster that this framework failed to identify. Also, we didn't find many differences between any of the five clusters of churches on faith-in-action behaviors like serving and evangelism (see Chart A.1). The differences between church types on levels of agreement with key Christian beliefs and engagement in personal spiritual practices also were not as meaningful as we expected. At this point, it was clear that by using only the Best Practice Principles, our categorization of churches relied solely on what a church brings to its congregants. This perspective is important, but it leaves out what

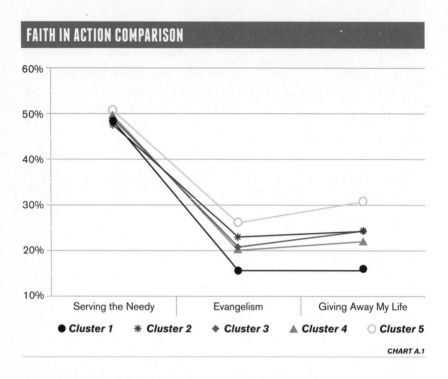

FAITH IN ACTION COMPARISON

● *Cluster 1*   ✳ *Cluster 2*   ◆ *Cluster 3*   ▲ *Cluster 4*   ○ *Cluster 5*

CHART A.1

the congregant brings to the church. We turned our attention to the catalysts next.

Coincidentally, as with the K-means clustering of churches based on the Best Practice Principles, a five-group solution based on the catalysts was determined to be the best. The catalyst framework led to large differences between clusters on the personal spiritual practices and faith-in-action variables, but less difference on the variable measuring satisfaction with church (see Charts A.2 and A.3). Furthermore, the percentage of congregants in each stage of the spiritual continuum did not differ much between three of the church types.

Like the best practices clustering, the catalyst clustering seemed incomplete as a framework for the archetypes. It captured differences between congregants fairly well but didn't tell us much about the relationship between these differences and the ways in which churches encourage spiritual growth. Making recommendations to

CHURCHES CLUSTERED BY CATALYSTS

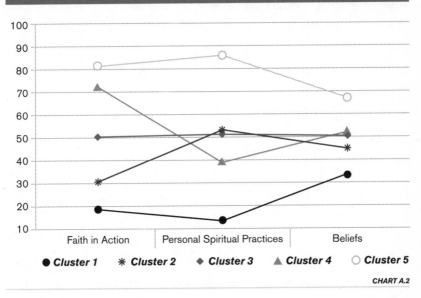

Faith in Action | Personal Spiritual Practices | Beliefs

● Cluster 1   ✳ Cluster 2   ◆ Cluster 3   ▲ Cluster 4   ○ Cluster 5

CHART A.2

THE CATALYST CLUSTERS WERE TOO SIMILAR ON THE BEST PRACTICES

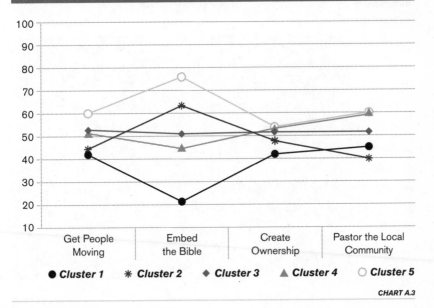

Get People Moving | Embed the Bible | Create Ownership | Pastor the Local Community

● Cluster 1   ✳ Cluster 2   ◆ Cluster 3   ▲ Cluster 4   ○ Cluster 5

CHART A.3

church leaders on how to get their churches moving toward greater spiritual vibrancy based on the catalyst framework only or the best practices framework only would be difficult. Given that being able to provide help to church leaders was the key goal of this project, it was clear that neither would work on its own.

STEP THREE: FINALIZING THE ARCHETYPES

At this point, we had two sets of clusters: one set formed using the best practices and one formed using the catalysts. The first produced groups that differed markedly in congregants' levels of satisfaction with the church and in their patterns of strengths and weaknesses on the Best Practice Principles. However, the groups did not show differences among congregants in their beliefs, personal spiritual practices, or faith in action in the ways we expected. The catalyst

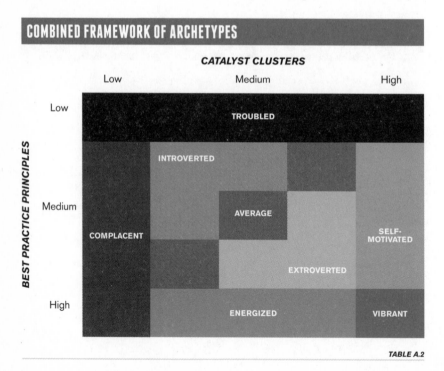

COMBINED FRAMEWORK OF ARCHETYPES

CATALYST CLUSTERS

BEST PRACTICE PRINCIPLES

	Low	Medium	High
Low		TROUBLED	
		INTROVERTED	
Medium	COMPLACENT	AVERAGE	SELF-MOTIVATED
		EXTROVERTED	
High		ENERGIZED	VIBRANT

TABLE A.2

clusters did show differences in these areas but did not vary much in their views of their church. It seemed to us that the strengths of one framework complemented the strengths of the other while canceling out the other's weaknesses. When we put the two frameworks together to create the 5x5 grid shown in Table A.2, the differences between each archetype crystalized. The combination provided the best overall means of sorting churches according to where they are on a continuum of spiritual vibrancy.

When we plot the percentile ranks for each archetype on the catalysts (Chart A.4) and the Best Practice Principles (Chart A.5), the differentiation achieved by this segmentation is clear. Charts A.4 and A.5 bring together the charts included in each of the archetype chapters in *Rise* to show the clear distinctions between them. They reveal some interesting patterns that point to the importance of considering both aspects of a church in determining its archetype and understanding how to help it succeed. For example, Self-Motivated

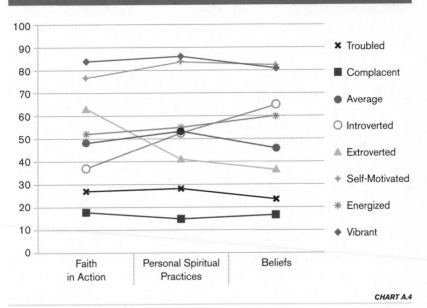

COMPARISON OF THE ARCHETYPES ON THE CATALYSTS

CHART A.4

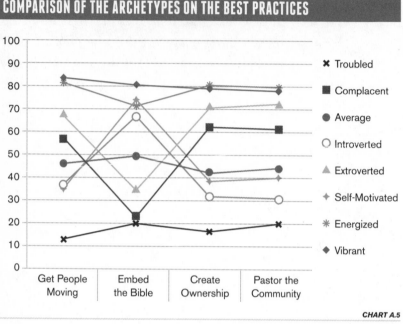

COMPARISON OF THE ARCHETYPES ON THE BEST PRACTICES

Legend:
- ✖ Troubled
- ■ Complacent
- ● Average
- ○ Introverted
- ▲ Extroverted
- ✦ Self-Motivated
- ✳ Energized
- ◆ Vibrant

X-axis: Get People Moving · Embed the Bible · Create Ownership · Pastor the Community

CHART A.5

Churches look similar to Vibrant Churches on the catalysts chart. But on the chart for the Best Practice Principles, Self-Motivated Churches have a pattern of results that differs distinctly from Vibrant Churches, with sharply lower scores across the board.

THE POWER OF PATTERNS

In the thirteenth century, an Italian mathematician named Fibonacci described a sequence of numbers that forms a pattern found widely in nature—in everything from the arrangement of fruit spouts on a pineapple to the pattern of leaves on a stem to the family trees of honeybees. This pattern, known as the Fibonacci sequence, is so useful that computer programmers have created algorithms based on it that allow computer memory to work faster and more efficiently.

That's the power of recognizing patterns in a set of data. Patterns bring order to seeming randomness and help us to better interpret the world around us. They allow us to see beneath the surface to understand how something works and how to make it even better. The driving force behind this project from the beginning was a deep desire to find patterns of churches so that we could help churches of every type to keep moving forward toward greater spiritual vibrancy. By sorting through the data and quantitatively validating the patterns that became the church archetypes, we hope to have activated the power of patterns to help every church maximize its potential for extending God's Kingdom and bringing hope to the world.

ACKNOWLEDGMENTS

Among the many people behind the work that led to *Rise*, a few stand out for their sacrificial efforts and support:

Willow Creek Community Church and the Willow Creek Association (WCA)
In 2004, God planted the seeds for REVEAL and *Rise* with Willow Creek's leaders—including senior pastor Bill Hybels, who believed "facts are your friends" and advocated the findings of REVEAL to thousands of churches around the world. We are also indebted to Greg Hawkins, former executive pastor of Willow Creek, who led the charge for the creation and funding of REVEAL—and to Jim Mellado, former president of the WCA, who nurtured and protected its development.

Eric Arnson
The marketplace genius behind REVEAL, Eric has dedicated a decade of energy and time (much of it pro bono) to advancing its work. Eric is a tireless champion of the local church, and *Rise* is a product of his humble service on its behalf.

Terry Schweizer
In 2007, Terry left the secular fruits of twenty years in market research for the full-time challenge of leading REVEAL's national and global expansion. While it is impossible to capture the impact of his role, it's comparable to that of a symphony conductor or an NFL coach, guiding many disparate resources to a harmonious and victorious end. Without him, REVEAL would not exist today—and *Rise* would never have been written.

Judy Keene
Judy is the REVEAL "whisperer"—our greatest ongoing source of editorial support and encouragement. Although her stellar writing credentials attract constant job offers from Christian and secular clients, the work of REVEAL is always at the top of her to-do list because she believes in its power to revitalize churches everywhere. *Rise* is a direct reflection of her expert guidance and handiwork.

Scott Beck
When REVEAL transitioned from Willow Creek to Scott's leadership, *Rise* was no more than an idea. There was no book proposal, no publisher, and no resource commitment to get it done. Any insights derived by church leaders from *Rise* are due entirely to Scott's personal, financial, and spiritual support.

REVEAL pastors
As dozens of stories in *Rise* attest, it takes leadership "guts" and spiritual fortitude to ask your congregants about the state of their relationship with Christ and the discipleship effectiveness of their church. We are deeply grateful to the thousands of church leaders who stepped up to that challenge, leading to the extraordinary insights that inspired *Rise*.

Randy Lewis and Rich Parkinson
Big 24/7 projects like book writing demand sacrifices at home. Thankfully, we are both blessed with uncomplaining husbands who not only shouldered the extra load due to our absence or distraction but also celebrated or consoled us whenever necessary. Randy and Rich, you are both greatly loved and much appreciated.

ABOUT THE AUTHORS

Cally Parkinson is the director for REVEAL, an initiative that utilizes research tools and discoveries to help churches better understand spiritual growth in their congregations. To date, REVEAL has served 2,000 churches and surveyed 500,000 congregants. Cally has coauthored four books with Willow Creek's former executive pastor, Greg Hawkins, describing the insights from REVEAL.

Cally previously served as the director of communications at Willow Creek Community Church, a role she took on following a twenty-five-year career at Allstate Insurance Company. At Allstate, she held a number of different director- and officer-level positions in strategic planning, research, finance, and communications. She has a BA in languages from DePauw University and a master's degree from the Thunderbird School of Global Management. Cally and her husband, Rich, live in the Chicago suburbs and have two grown children (plus two adorable grandchildren).

Nancy Scammacca Lewis joined the REVEAL team as lead statistician in 2008. She is an ordained deacon in the Anglican Church in North America and served on the pastoral staff of two church plants for more than ten years. In addition to her work with REVEAL,

Nancy conducts research projects in education and the social sciences. Her work has been published in several major education research journals. She holds a PhD in quantitative methods from the University of Texas at Austin, a master's degree from Wheaton College, and a bachelor's degree from Northwestern University. Nancy and her husband, Randy, live in the Chicago suburbs.

TAKE YOUR NEXT STEP

Discover *your* church's personality.

Lead for transformation.

Help your church RISE.

Learn what REVEAL can do for your church
and the people you love to lead.

Begin your archetype-discovery journey at:

www.REVEAL4US.com

CP0934

NAVIGATOR **CHURCH** MINISTRIES

NCM focuses on helping churches become more intentional in discipleship and outreach. NCM staff help pastors, church leaders, and lifelong laborers across the United States develop an effective and personalized approach to accomplishing the Great Commission.

NCM works alongside the local church to grow intentional disciple-making cultures, as reflected in the following illustration:

Growing *intentional* Disciplemaking Cultures
A process to help churches send laborers into their communities

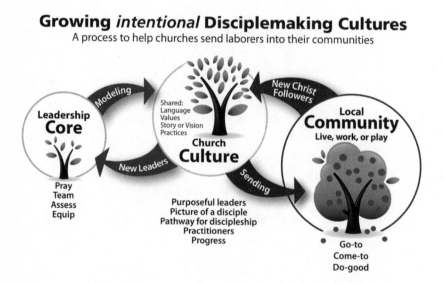

NCM also offers seminars, materials, and coaching to help the local church see discipleship flourish in successive generations. See our web page for further information on how NCM can help you.

www.navigatorchurchministries.org
Call our NCM Office at (719) 594-2446
or write to PO Box 6000, Colorado Springs, CO 80934